QUICK & DELICIOUS

SPECIAL DELIGHTS

BATTERED, COVERED OR WRAPPED!

by

Johna Blinn

Edited by Tom Dorsey

**Published by Playmore Inc., Publishers and Waldman Publishing Corp.,
New York, New York**

Printed in Canada/Cover Printed in the United States of America

Edited by Malvina G. Vogel

*Cover Photo: Gordon E. Smith:
courtesy Family Circle Great Ideas*

Acknowledgments

This writer is especially indebted to the expert advice, encouragement and cooperation of many. I am particularly indebted to Ruth Lundgren, Olive Dempsey, A.C. Collins, Yvonne Martin, Lois Westlund, Mary Hoban, Marjorie Z. Ashby, Pat Mason, Dodie Sway, Chris Pines, Caryl Saunders, Anita Fial, Anita Mizner, Claire Boasi, Marlys Bielunski, Keamette Cheng, Fresh Garlic Association, Imported Winter Grape Association, Planter's Peanut Oil, Tuna Research Foundation, Florida Citrus Commission, Lea & Perrins Worcestershire Sauce, Lawrys Foods, Inc., Stokely-Van Camp, Inc., United Fresh Fruit and Vegetable Association, American Spice Trade Association, Karo Corn Syrup, Mrs. Cubbison's Foods, Inc., Angostura International Ltd., North American Blueberry Council, Del Monte Kitchens, Fleischmann's Active Dry Yeast, National Livestock & Meat Board, Campbell Soup Co., McIlhenny Co., South African Rock Lobster Service Association, American Lamb Council, Blue Bonnet Margarine, Nabisco, Inc. and Dubonnet Blanc.

J.B.

BARONET
BOOKS

BARONET BOOKS is a trademark of Playmore Inc., Publishers
and Waldman Publishing Corp., New York, N.Y.

Copyright © MCMLXXXVII by Johna Blinn. All rights reserved. No part of this cookbook may be used or reproduced in any manner whatsoever without written permission except in the case of brief quotations embodied in critical articles and reviews. For information or permission write to Waldman Publishing Corp., 18 East 41st Street, New York, N.Y. 10017.

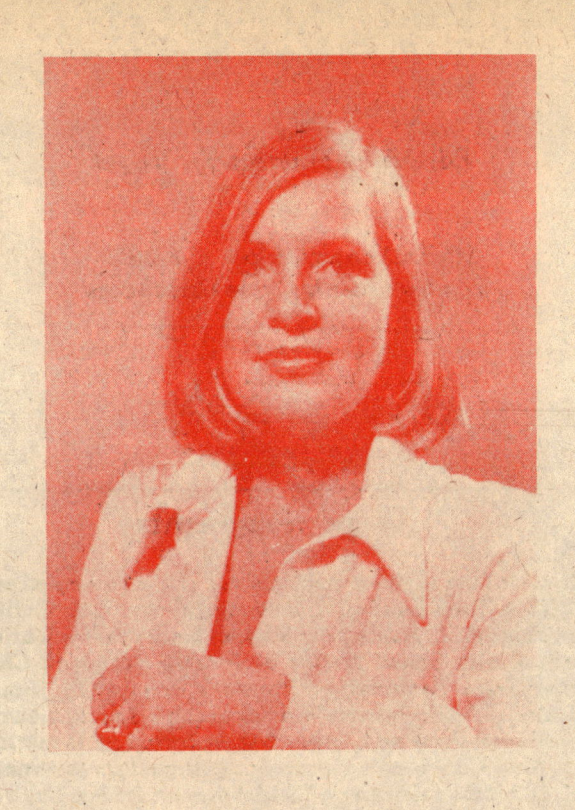

The Author

To many of the top movie and television stars, Johna Blinn is a celebrity. For almost 20 years they have welcomed her into their homes, onto sets, just about anywhere to talk about food, entertaining and lifestyles. Her column, "Celebrity Cookbook," is syndicated throughout the world and appears weekly in more than 140 newspapers and periodicals. A collection of hundreds of these conversations and recipes appears in *Celebrity Cookbook*, published by Waldman Publishing Corporation. Currently, Johna Blinn is writing a series on Celebrity Food-styles for *FAMILY CIRCLE*, America's largest supermarket magazine (circulation, 20 million), where she has already profiled Tom Brokaw, Angela Lansbury, John Madden, Michael Landon, Robert Urich, Raymond Burr, Steve Garvey, Diane Sawyer and others.

Blinn is a former assistant food editor of LOOK magazine and is the author of a number of books, including *The Shangri-la Cookbook, Fabulous Appetizers, Fabulous Soups, Fabulous Salads, Fabulous Vegetarian Recipes, Fabulous Poultry & Game, Fabulous Meats, Fabulous Fish & Seafood, Fabulous Desserts, Fabulous Low Calorie Recipes, Fabulous Oriental Recipes, Fabulous Oven & Stovetop Recipes*, and *Fabulous Italian Recipes*, all published by Waldman Publishing Corporation. In addition, Blinn is a frequent contributor of up close and personal interviews, profiles and entertainment features to *USA TODAY* and other American and foreign newspapers and magazines.

A graduate of the State University of Iowa, Blinn took graduate work in Home Economics at the University of Wisconsin and taught home economics in Iowa, Virginia and New York. Now based in Los Angeles, she is married to a nationally known newspaper syndicate editor, writer and management consultant, and they have two grown children.

Introduction

SPECIAL DELIGHTS, Battered, Covered or Wrapped presents a wonderful way to cook foods "under cover." Cooking anything "under cover" means anything that is battered, covered or wrapped, be it in foil or a delightfully flaky biscuit or pie dough. Any way you do it, under cover can prove to be a new, unique, economical way to present leftovers, extend small bits of expensive food, or just a novel way to present food favorites such as sandwiches in a mystery loaf (bread loaf hollowed out and filled with a tasty meat concoction to slice for lunch, supper or snacking.)

Foods are commonly prepared under cover in foreign countries. For example, there are delicious chicken or beef tacos from our neighbors south of the border. Tortilla-wrapped tacos and burritos are fast becoming an intrinsic part of the American diet. Batter-fried empanadas—tiny chicken, fish or vegetable turnovers sold by Argentinian street vendors or created by home cooks—are as popular there as hot dogs and hamburgers are here.

From England, we've borrowed Cornish pasties—crescent-shaped turnovers fashioned from meat or chicken encased and baked in a flaky pastry. For centuries, Cornish housewives have been making them for their coal-miner husbands for lunch. Turnovers or pinwheels are common ways to create anything from tiny appetizers to main dish fare.

Italian cooks have a genius for combining a small amount of meat, fowl or fish with pastry or pasta. For example, they create ravioli or tortellini filled with cheese or meat, to cook in soup, or as the basis for a casserole, covered with a delicious marinara sauce.

Eastern European cooks have long been famous for their stuffed cabbage rolls.

From the French, we've learned the sophisticated way to bake pâté in pastry or filet wrapped in pastry in a creation the English call Beef Wellington. No one's quite certain how the famous dish got its name Wellington. Several theories have been advanced. For example, it's been said that the dish was invented by a chef at a restaurant in Wellington, England. A more romantic version has the dish being developed in honor of the Duke on the occasion of one of his myriad steps up the military and political ladder. Since he was known to have bought most of his promotions, perhaps some cuisinier with a wry humor thought to "cover up" the traditional roast beef with pastry. At any rate, the dish is dramatic. And the idea of putting a Wellington coat over fillings other than beef has become as popular in gourmet circles as with everyday cooks.

Filled or stuffed fowl, meat or fish has always been a delightfully simple but delicious way to present a main dish. This way, the cook can extend expensive meat or fish by using a herb-pungent mixture. The Germans do this as rouladen, choosing a thin slice of steak and filling it with a bread dressing. Stuffed vegetables such as moussaka—lamb or beef-filled eggplants from the Middle East—create a delightful make-ahead main dish for servantless hosts or hostesses. In fact, that's part of the appeal of under-cover cooking: most of the cooking and dishwashing is done in advance.

Under cover need not be limited to hors d'oeuvres or entrées. Crêpes or blintzes, for example, make a delightful conclusion as desserts for lunch or brunch. The golden lacy pancakes can be filled with anything as delightful as fresh strawberries in season to a kosher lunch of cheese blintzes.

Any way you do it—batter-frying corn dogs for a backyard cookout, or preparing and stuffing your favorite vegetables with new fillings, or treating your family to such classics as shepherd pie or deep dish meat pies—cooking under cover is certain to tickle your fancy and delight your family or guests and help you stay within your budget. With a little ingenuity and practice, you will soon find yourself inventing new ways to prepare old family favorite recipes "under cover."

J.B.

CONTENTS

OPENERS

Puff-Top Tuna Bisque	7
Knaidlach (for Soup)	7
Brie in Walnut Pastry	8
Tuna-Spinach Falafel with Savory Sauce	8
Empanadas	9
Crab-Stuffed Mushrooms	10
Chang's Pork in Lettuce	10

MAINDISH FARE

FISH

Crab-Filled Cheese Puffs with Seafood Sauce	11
Baked Fish Packets	12
Flounder Florentine	12
Rock Lobster in Pasta Shells	13
Rock Lobster-Filled Pancakes	13
Shrimp-Stuffed Fish Fillets	14
Stuffed Baked Fish with Gourmet Tomato Sauce	14
Salmon-Spinach Turnovers	15
Sweet & Sour Shrimp in the Shell	16
Rock Lobster Wellington	16
Salmon-Filled Crêpes	17
Baked Snapper with Sour Cream Stuffing	18
Tuna Dutch Baby with Tuna-Vegetable Filling	18
Moussaka di Mare	19

BEEF

Beef Roll-Ups with Sausage	20
Peachy Beef Pinwheel	20
Corn-Stuffed Beef Birds	21
Stuffed Beef Rolls with Sherried Asparagus Sauce	21
Milano Beef Torte	22
Beef Wellington	22
Burger Turnovers	23
Olive's Cornish Pasties	23
Cannelloni	24
Beef Dolmades	24
Dilled Cabbage Rolls	25
Beef & Barley Cabbage Rolls	26
Swedish Cabbage Rolls	26
Lasagna Roll-Ups	27
Machaca de Huevos	27
Blanketed Beef Loaf	28
Carrie's Cabbage Meat Loaf	28
Carrot-Stuffed Meat Loaf	29
Meat Loaf Roll-Up, American Style	29
Italian Tortilla Snacks	30
Angostura Minute Steaks	30
Rouladen	31

BEEF (cont.)

Flank Steak, Creole Style	31
Steak Roll-Ups	32
Vegetable Pie	32
Beanpot o' Gold	33
Corn Dogs 'n Beans	33
Dieter's Shepherd's Pie	33

LAMB

Stuffed Lamb Chop Special	34
Lamb Rolls	34
Stuffed Breast of Lamb	35
Lamb-Asparagus Rolls	35
Lamb Chops in Jackets	35

PORK

Sweet Potato-Stuffed Pork Chops	36
Texas Burritos	36
Fruit-Stuffed Pork Loin	37
Sadie's Ham & 'Tater Stack	37
Pork-Stuffed Cabbage Rolls	38
Fruit-Stuffed Pork Roast	38
Pork Shoulder with Grapefruit Stuffing	39
Finnish Pork Pot Pie	39
Angostura Lasagna Rolls	40
Roly-Poly Pork Loaves with Corn Bread Stuffing	40
Swiss Vegetable Roll with Mustard Sauce	41
Tasty Pork Turnovers	42
Sausage Links in Batter Pudding	42
Roasted Potatoes & Sausage Under Wraps	43
Stuffed Pork Butterfly Chops	43

POULTRY

Foiled Chicken Supreme	44
Sherried Chicken-Filled Crêpes	44
Tortellini	45

MAINDISH FARE (cont.)

POULTRY (cont.)

Chicken Breasts Stuffed with Herb Wheat Germ	46
Folded Stuffed Chicken with Lemon Barbecue Sauce	46
Cannelloni Supreme	47
Avocado Chicken Breasts	48
Chicken Flautas with Guacamole con Cilantro	48
Vegetable-Chicken Pockets	49
Mexican Chicken Kiev	50
Mexican Rolls	50
Mom's Chicken Croquettes with Peas	51
Mom's Turkey Pie	51

VEGETARIAN DISHES

Stuffed Artichokes	52
Cheese-Filled Pasta Shells	52
Bo-Peep Pie	53
Zesty Cheese Strata	53
Eggs McMorice	54
Parisian Soufflé Roll-Up	54
Sam's Potato-Stuffed Omelet	55
Chile Rellenos	56
Tangy Broiled Tomato Halves	56
Orange Shell Squash	56
Stuffed Tomatoes	57
Stuffed Peppers, Angostura	57
Wheat Germ Ravioli with Spinach Filling	58
Spinach-Zucchini Boats	59
Foiled Vegetable Toss, Grilled	59
Curry-Stuffed Onions	60
Baked Stuffed Zucchini	60
Bean-Stuffed Tomatoes	61
Elsie's Eggplant Supreme	61

SALADS

Tuna Nicosia	62
Winter Grape & Seafood Salad with Chili Dressing	62
Mexicali Corn Salad with Salsa Olé	63

FINGER FOOD

Calzone	64
Falafel Patties	64
Quarterback's Crescent Franks	65
Peel Deals	65
Deviled Corned Beef Buns	65
Ham en Panier	66
Mexican Monte Carlo Sandwich	66
Monte Cristo Sandwich	67
Ramada	67
Pâté en Croute	67
Mystery Loaf	68
Beef Loaf in a Loaf	68
Sausage Pockets	69
Nan's Nutty Pita Pockets	69
Fried Reuben Sandwiches	69
Crêpe Sandwich Torte with Sour Cream Mustard Sauce	70
Florentine Submarines	70
Taco Crescents	71
Ensaimada Rolls	71
Walnut Honey Buns	72

DESSERTS

Cheese Blintzes	73
Ambrosia Pizza	73
Strawberry Crêpes	74
Pineapple Cake Roll	74
Blueberry Roll	75
Mona's Walnut Florentines	76
Nut-Filled Pastries	76
Dessert Fruit Tacos	77
Spicy Applesauce Ice Cream Roll	77
Dubonnet Golden Tart	78
Raisin Star Cookies	78
Cheese-Date Fold-Overs	79
Angel Waldorf Delight	80
Baked Alaska	80

Puff-Top Tuna Bisque

Serves 6

- 1 package (10 ounces) frozen creamed spinach, thawed
- 1 cup chicken or vegetable broth
- 2 cups milk
- ½ cup grated Parmesan cheese
- 2 tablespoons chopped chives
- 1 teaspoon dried leaf basil
- ½ teaspoon salt
- ¼ teaspoon pepper
- 1 can (6½ or 7 ounces) tuna
- 6 frozen patty shells (10-ounce package), defrosted
- 1 egg

1. Combine spinach and chicken broth in an electric blender; process until smooth.
2. Add milk, cheese, chives, basil, salt and pepper.
3. Divide tuna equally among 6 ovenproof 1½-cup soup bowls; pour soup mixture into bowls.
4. Using a rolling pin, roll each patty shell into a 6-inch circle.
5. Gently lay pastry over top of soup bowls, leaving 1-inch overhang; seal by pressing firmly to sides of bowl (do not crimp to rim; pastry must be allowed to rise freely).
6. Lightly beat egg; brush all pastry tops.
7. Position oven rack in lower third of oven.
8. Bake bisque in preheated 400° F. oven 10 to 15 minutes, or until pastry is puffed and golden brown.
9. Serve immediately; to eat, break up pastry dome with spoon and stir into soup. (It will become thickened and creamy.)

Knaidlach (for Soup)

Makes about 18 matzo balls

- ⅓ cup peanut oil
- ½ cup minced onion
- 2 eggs, separated
- ⅓ cup cold water
- 1 teaspoon salt
- ⅛ teaspoon pepper
- 2 tablespoons chopped parsley
- ⅔ cup matzo meal
- boiling chicken soup or salted water

1. Heat peanut oil in a saucepan; cook onion until tender in hot oil.
2. Remove onion from heat.
3. Beat together egg yolks, cold water, salt and pepper; gradually beat in onions until completely blended.
4. Stir in chopped parsley and matzo meal.
5. Beat egg whites until stiff peaks form; gradually fold into matzo meal mixture.
6. Cover and chill in refrigerator at least 1 hour.
7. Using 2 teaspoons, measure rounded teaspoons of matzo meal mixture; shape into balls and drop into boiling chicken soup or salted water.
8. Cover and cook knaidlach in simmering liquid 25 to 30 minutes.
9. Serve with hot soup.

NOTE: Knaidlach have long been a favorite accessory for soup.

OPENERS

Brie in Walnut Pastry

Makes two 6-inch rounds

1½ cups all-purpose flour
½ cup chopped walnuts
⅔ cup margarine
3 to 4 tablespoons ice water
2 packages (4½ ounces) Brie cheese

1. Combine flour and walnuts; cut in margarine until mixture resembles coarse meal.
2. Stir in water to form a soft dough; divide dough into quarters.
3. On a lightly floured surface, pat or roll each quarter into a 6-inch circle.
4. Place each Brie on a circle of dough; top with remaining circles, crimping edges securely to seal.
5. Bake in preheated 425° F. oven 20 to 25 minutes, until pastry is light golden brown.
6. Let stand 30 minutes before serving.

NOTE: For Gouda in Pastry, substitute two 8-ounce packages Gouda cheese for Brie.

Tuna-Spinach Falafel with Savory Sauce

Makes about 36 falafel (6 servings)

1 can (1 pound 4 ounces) chick peas, drained, reserve ½ cup liquid
1 package (10 ounces) frozen chopped spinach, thawed
2 cans (6½ or 7 ounces each) tuna in vegetable oil
½ cup chopped onion
½ cup packaged dry bread crumbs
2 tablespoons chopped parsley
1 egg, lightly beaten
2 cloves garlic, minced
1 teaspoon ground coriander
¼ to ½ teaspoon cayenne pepper
vegetable oil for frying
6 large pita bread
Savory Sauce
1 tomato, chopped
1 cucumber, chopped
shredded lettuce

1. Purée chick peas with ½ cup reserved liquid from can in an electric blender; cover and process until smooth. Turn into a bowl.
2. Drain spinach thoroughly by pressing in a sieve with the back of a large spoon; add to chick pea purée.
3. Drain tuna of excess liquid; flake finely with a fork.
4. Add tuna to purée mixture.
5. Blend in onion, bread crumbs, parsley, egg, garlic, coriander and cayenne; cover and chill 1 hour.
6. Shape mixture into small balls about ¾ inch in diameter.
7. Heat oil in a large skillet; brown falafel balls on all sides, over medium heat (about 10 minutes total frying time).
8. Drain well on paper toweling.

9. Serve in heated pita bread topped with Savory Sauce, chopped tomato, cucumber and shredded lettuce.

Savory Sauce

Makes ⅔ cup sauce

⅓ cup mayonnaise   ⅓ cup catsup

Mix together both ingredients in a small bowl.

Empanadas
(Argentine Beef Turnovers)

Serves 12

- 1 package (8 ounces) cream cheese, softened
- ½ cup butter or margarine, softened
- 1½ cups all-purpose flour
- 1 tablespoon olive or salad oil
- 2 tablespoons minced onion
- ½ pound ground lean beef
- 1 can (8¼ ounces) tomatoes, drained and crushed
- 2 tablespoons chopped raisins
- 2 tablespoons chopped pitted green olives
- 1 tablespoon original Worcestershire sauce
- ½ teaspoon salt
- ½ teaspoon oregano leaves, crumbled
- 1 hard-cooked egg, chopped
- 1 egg yolk
- 1 tablespoon water
- ¼ cup sesame seed

1. Blend together cream cheese and butter in the large bowl of an electric mixer.
2. Gradually add flour; blend until dough is smooth.
3. Divide dough into 3 balls; cover and chill until firm, about 30 minutes.
4. Heat oil in a medium-size skillet; add onion and sauté 3 minutes.
5. Add meat; cook and stir until browned, about 5 minutes.
6. Stir in tomatoes, raisins, olives, Worcestershire sauce, salt and oregano; simmer, uncovered, 5 minutes, stirring often.
7. Stir in chopped egg; cool.
8. On a lightly floured board, roll each ball of dough separately to ⅛-inch thickness; cut out 3-inch circles.
9. Spoon 1 teaspoon meat mixture onto one-half of each circle.
10. Moisten pastry edges with water; fold over filling to form a semi-circle.
11. Press edges to seal; crimp with fork tines.
12. Prick tops of turnovers to allow steam to escape.
13. Mix egg yolk with water; brush over tops of turnovers.
14. Sprinkle with sesame seed.
15. Place turnovers on cookie sheets; bake in preheated 400° F. oven until golden, about 12 minutes.

OPENERS

Crab-Stuffed Mushrooms

Makes 24 stuffed mushrooms

- 1 pound large mushrooms (about 24)
- ¼ cup chopped onion
- ¼ cup margarine
- 15 Ritz crackers, finely rolled (about ¾ cup crumbs)
- 1 package (6 ounces) frozen crab meat, thawed and drained
- 1 jar (2 ounces) diced pimientos, undrained
- 2 teaspoons horseradish
- ⅛ teaspoon ground black pepper

1. Remove stems from mushroom caps; arrange caps on baking sheet.
2. Finely chop stems.
3. Sauté mushroom stems and onion in margarine in a skillet until tender.
4. Stir in remaining ingredients.
5. Spoon about 1 tablespoon crab mixture into each cap.
6. Bake in preheated 350° F. oven 20 to 25 minutes, or until done.

Chang's Pork in Lettuce

Serves 4

- 1 large head lettuce or 2 heads Boston lettuce
- 6 to 8 Chinese dried black mushrooms (optional)
- boiling water (optional)
- 1 can (8 ounces) water chestnuts, drained and minced
- ½ cup bamboo shoots, drained and minced
- 1 pound ground pork
- 1 egg, lightly beaten
- 1½ tablespoons soy sauce
- 1 tablespoon plus 1 teaspoon cornstarch
- 2 tablespoons dry sherry
- ½ cup chicken broth
- 1 teaspoon salt
- ¼ cup corn oil

1 cup minced celery

1. Cut lettuce in half.
2. Arrange 16 to 20 of the largest leaves on a serving dish; refrigerate.
3. Soak mushrooms in boiling water to cover for 30 minutes. Drain; cut off stems.
4. Add water chestnuts and bamboo shoots to mushrooms; set aside.
5. Mix together pork, egg, soy sauce and 1 tablespoon cornstarch; set aside.
6. Combine sherry, ½ cup chicken broth and salt; blend remaining cornstarch with remaining chicken broth.
7. Heat oil in a wok; add pork mixture and cook, stirring constantly, 5 minutes.
8. Add mushroom mixture; cook, stirring, 2 minutes longer.
9. Stir in wine and cornstarch mixtures.
10. Add celery; stir until celery is heated through.
11. Place meat mixture in a serving dish.
12. To serve, let diners select lettuce leaf, fill with pork mixture, and roll to eat with fingers.

Crab-Filled Cheese Puffs with Seafood Sauce

Serves 6

½ cup water
2 tablespoons butter
¼ teaspoon salt
½ cup flour
1 tablespoon cornstarch
1 cup (4 ounces) shredded Cheddar cheese
2 eggs

1. Combine water, butter and salt in a 1-quart saucepan; heat to a boil.
2. Add flour and cornstarch all at once; stir vigorously over low heat until mixture leaves sides of pan and forms a smooth, compact mass.
3. Remove from heat and add cheese; stir until cheese is melted.
4. Transfer dough into a small mixing bowl; add eggs, 1 at a time, beating until smooth and glossy after each addition.
5. Chill 1 hour.
6. Mound dough into 6 portions on buttered baking sheet; bake in preheated 450° F. oven 15 minutes.
7. Reduce heat to 350° F.; bake 30 minutes longer.
8. Cut a small slit in side of each puff to allow steam to escape; remove to wire rack to cool.
9. Cut off tops of puffs.

Seafood Sauce

2 tablespoons chopped celery
2 tablespoons grated onion
3 tablespoons butter
3 tablespoons flour
1½ cups milk
1 package (10 ounces) frozen peas
1 can (5 ounces) crab meat, rinsed and drained
1 can (4¼ ounces) medium shrimp, rinsed and drained
1 teaspoon fresh lemon juice
1 teaspoon original Worcestershire sauce
¼ teaspoon salt
¾ cup shredded Cheddar cheese

1. Sauté celery and onion in butter until tender, about 5 minutes; stir in flour.
2. Remove from heat; gradually stir in milk.
3. Return to heat and cook, stirring constantly, until thickened; cook 2 minutes longer.
4. Add peas, crab meat, shrimp, lemon juice, Worcestershire sauce and salt; heat to serving temperature.
5. Remove from heat; add cheese, stirring until melted. (If necessary, return to low heat to melt cheese. Do not boil.)
6. Keep warm.
7. To serve, heat Cheese Puffs in 350° F. oven 5 to 10 minutes; fill with seafood sauce and serve at once.

Baked Fish Packets

Serves 4

- 2 tablespoons water
- 8 ounces fresh mushrooms, chopped
- ½ teaspoon oregano leaves, crushed
- ¼ cup dry white wine
- 1 tablespoon lemon juice
- 1 teaspoon onion powder
- ¼ teaspoon salt
- 1/16 teaspoon ground black pepper
- 4 flounder fillets (4 ounces each)
- 1 teaspoon parsley flakes
- ¼ teaspoon paprika
- 4 thin lemon slices

1. Bring water to a boil in a small skillet.
2. Add mushrooms and oregano; cook, stirring, over moderate heat until tender, about 5 minutes.
3. Add wine and lemon juice; cook, stirring, until almost all of the liquid evaporates, about 2 minutes.
4. Stir in onion powder, salt and black pepper; remove from heat.
5. Lightly grease four 12-inch squares of foil; place a fillet on each piece of foil.
6. Top each fillet with an equal portion of mushroom mixture; sprinkle each with parsley flakes and paprika; top with a lemon slice.
7. Draw edges of foil together and seal; place on a baking sheet.
8. Bake in preheated 400° F. oven just until fish turns opaque, about 20 minutes.

Flounder Florentine

Serves 6

- ¼ cup minced onion
- ⅛ teaspoon crushed rosemary
- 2 tablespoons butter or margarine
- 1 package (9½ ounces) frozen chopped spinach, cooked and well-drained
- ½ cup cooked rice
- ¼ cup chopped toasted almonds
- 1 tablespoon fresh lemon juice
- 6 fresh fillets of flounder (about 1½ pounds)
- 1 can (10¾ ounces) condensed cream of mushroom soup
- ¼ cup water
- paprika

1. Cook onion and rosemary in butter in a saucepan until tender.
2. Add spinach, rice, almonds and lemon juice; heat, stirring occasionally.
3. Place ¼ cup mixture on each fillet; roll up and secure with toothpicks.
4. Arrange roll-ups in a shallow 12 × 8 × 2-inch baking dish.
5. Bake in preheated 350° F. oven 20 minutes.
6. Meanwhile, blend together soup and water; pour over fish, stirring around sides.
7. Bake 15 minutes longer, or until done.
8. Stir sauce before serving; sprinkle with paprika.

Crab-Filled Cheese Puffs with Seafood Sauce

Serves 6

½ cup water
2 tablespoons butter
¼ teaspoon salt
½ cup flour
1 tablespoon cornstarch
1 cup (4 ounces) shredded Cheddar cheese
2 eggs

1. Combine water, butter and salt in a 1-quart saucepan; heat to a boil.
2. Add flour and cornstarch all at once; stir vigorously over low heat until mixture leaves sides of pan and forms a smooth, compact mass.
3. Remove from heat and add cheese; stir until cheese is melted.
4. Transfer dough into a small mixing bowl; add eggs, 1 at a time, beating until smooth and glossy after each addition.
5. Chill 1 hour.
6. Mound dough into 6 portions on buttered baking sheet; bake in preheated 450° F. oven 15 minutes.
7. Reduce heat to 350° F.; bake 30 minutes longer.
8. Cut a small slit in side of each puff to allow steam to escape; remove to wire rack to cool.
9. Cut off tops of puffs.

Seafood Sauce

2 tablespoons chopped celery
2 tablespoons grated onion
3 tablespoons butter
3 tablespoons flour
1½ cups milk
1 package (10 ounces) frozen peas
1 can (5 ounces) crab meat, rinsed and drained
1 can (4¼ ounces) medium shrimp, rinsed and drained
1 teaspoon fresh lemon juice
1 teaspoon original Worcestershire sauce
¼ teaspoon salt
¾ cup shredded Cheddar cheese

1. Sauté celery and onion in butter until tender, about 5 minutes; stir in flour.
2. Remove from heat; gradually stir in milk.
3. Return to heat and cook, stirring constantly, until thickened; cook 2 minutes longer.
4. Add peas, crab meat, shrimp, lemon juice, Worcestershire sauce and salt; heat to serving temperature.
5. Remove from heat; add cheese, stirring until melted. (If necessary, return to low heat to melt cheese. Do not boil.)
6. Keep warm.
7. To serve, heat Cheese Puffs in 350° F. oven 5 to 10 minutes; fill with seafood sauce and serve at once.

MAINDISH FARE　　　　　　　　　　　　　　　　　　　　　　　　　　　　　FISH

Baked Fish Packets

Serves 4

- 2 tablespoons water
- 8 ounces fresh mushrooms, chopped
- ½ teaspoon oregano leaves, crushed
- ¼ cup dry white wine
- 1 tablespoon lemon juice
- 1 teaspoon onion powder
- ¼ teaspoon salt
- ¹⁄₁₆ teaspoon ground black pepper
- 4 flounder fillets (4 ounces each)
- 1 teaspoon parsley flakes
- ¼ teaspoon paprika
- 4 thin lemon slices

1. Bring water to a boil in a small skillet.
2. Add mushrooms and oregano; cook, stirring, over moderate heat until tender, about 5 minutes.
3. Add wine and lemon juice; cook, stirring, until almost all of the liquid evaporates, about 2 minutes.
4. Stir in onion powder, salt and black pepper; remove from heat.
5. Lightly grease four 12-inch squares of foil; place a fillet on each piece of foil.
6. Top each fillet with an equal portion of mushroom mixture; sprinkle each with parsley flakes and paprika; top with a lemon slice.
7. Draw edges of foil together and seal; place on a baking sheet.
8. Bake in preheated 400° F. oven just until fish turns opaque, about 20 minutes.

Flounder Florentine

Serves 6

- ¼ cup minced onion
- ⅛ teaspoon crushed rosemary
- 2 tablespoons butter or margarine
- 1 package (9½ ounces) frozen chopped spinach, cooked and well-drained
- ½ cup cooked rice
- ¼ cup chopped toasted almonds
- 1 tablespoon fresh lemon juice
- 6 fresh fillets of flounder (about 1½ pounds)
- 1 can (10¾ ounces) condensed cream of mushroom soup
- ¼ cup water
- paprika

1. Cook onion and rosemary in butter in a saucepan until tender.
2. Add spinach, rice, almonds and lemon juice; heat, stirring occasionally.
3. Place ¼ cup mixture on each fillet; roll up and secure with toothpicks.
4. Arrange roll-ups in a shallow 12 × 8 × 2-inch baking dish.
5. Bake in preheated 350° F. oven 20 minutes.
6. Meanwhile, blend together soup and water; pour over fish, stirring around sides.
7. Bake 15 minutes longer, or until done.
8. Stir sauce before serving; sprinkle with paprika.

Rock Lobster in Pasta Shells

Serves 6

1 package (5 ounces) giant pasta shells
boiling salted water
3 packages (8 ounces each) South African rock lobster tails
¼ cup butter or margarine
½ cup chopped celery
½ cup chopped onion
1 clove garlic, chopped
1 egg
1½ cups (12 ounces) ricotta or cottage cheese
¼ cup grated Parmesan cheese
salt to taste
pepper to taste
2 cups (16 ounces) spaghetti sauce (canned or homemade)
¼ cup melted butter or margarine
½ cup dry bread crumbs

1. Cook shells in boiling salted water until tender but still firm; drain and cover with cold water to prevent sticking.
2. Thaw tails slightly; with scissors remove underside membrane, pull out meat and chop it.
3. Melt butter; sauté celery, onion and garlic until golden and tender.
4. Add rock lobster meat; sauté until white and opaque. Cool.
5. Beat in egg, ricotta and Parmesan cheeses; season to taste with salt and pepper.
6. Use mixture to stuff well-drained and dried pasta shells.
7. Pour spaghetti sauce into a greased shallow casserole; place shells, side by side, in a single layer into sauce.
8. Combine butter and crumbs; sprinkle over shells.
9. Bake in preheated 375° F. oven 30 to 35 minutes, or until lightly browned and hot.

Rock Lobster-Filled Pancakes

Serves 8

6 South African rock lobster tails, weighing 3 ounces each
boiling salted water
2 tablespoons butter
2 tablespoons flour
¾ cup milk
½ teaspoon scraped onion
1 can (8½ ounces) peas, drained
2 slices chopped pimiento
8 pancakes

1. Cook lobster tails in boiling salted water 3 minutes; drain immediately and drench with cold water.
2. Remove meat from shell; dice into small pieces.
3. Melt butter in a saucepan; blend in flour.
4. Add milk gradually; stir and cook until thickened.
5. Add onion, peas and pimiento.
6. Make individual pancakes from homemade batter or mix.
7. Place creamed rock lobster mixture on each pancake; roll up or fold in half.

Shrimp-Stuffed Fish Fillets

Serves 6 to 8

- 3 tablespoons butter or margarine
- ½ cup minced celery
- 3 tablespoons minced onion
- 1 can (4½ ounces) medium shrimp
- 1½ cups soft bread crumbs
- 1 egg, lightly beaten
- 4 teaspoons original Worcestershire sauce
- 6 to 8 (2 pounds) fillets of sole or flounder
- 1 can (10¾ ounces) condensed cream of shrimp soup
- ¼ cup milk
- 1 tablespoon chopped parsley

1. Melt butter in a small skillet; add celery and onion and sauté until tender, about 5 minutes.
2. Drain and rinse shrimp, reserving ¼ cup shrimp for sauce; finely chop remaining shrimp.
3. Combine shrimp with celery and onion in a small bowl.
4. Stir in bread crumbs, egg and 3 teaspoons Worcestershire sauce; mix well.
5. Place 1 heaping tablespoon of stuffing on each fillet; roll tightly and fasten with a toothpick if necessary.
6. Place fish rolls in an 11 × 7½ × 2-inch baking pan; set aside.
7. Combine soup, milk and parsley with reserved ¼ cup shrimp and remaining Worcestershire sauce in a small saucepan, mixing well; heat only until hot.
8. Pour sauce over fish rolls; cover and bake in preheated 350° F. oven until fish flakes easily when tested with a fork, about 40 minutes.

Stuffed Baked Fish with Gourmet Tomato Sauce

Serves 8

- seasoned salt
- 1 whole fish (red snapper, sea bass, trout or salmon, weighing 3 to 4 pounds dressed weight, boned and with cavity
- 1 recipe Stuffing
- ¼ cup melted butter or margarine
- 1 recipe Gourmet Tomato Sauce

1. Sprinkle seasoned salt in cavity of fish.
2. Pack stuffing lightly in cavity; fasten openings with picks or skewers and lace with string.
3. Place fish in greased shallow baking pan; brush with melted butter and sprinkle with seasoned salt.
4. Bake, uncovered, in preheated 350° F. oven about 1 hour, or until fish flakes easily.
5. Serve with Gourmet Tomato Sauce.

Stuffing

Makes 4 cups

¼ cup butter or margarine
½ cup minced onions
4 cups small dry bread cubes
¼ cup minced parsley
1 cup shredded carrots
2 teaspoons seasoned salt

1. Melt butter in skillet; sauté onions.
2. Place bread cubes in a bowl; add sautéed onions and remaining ingredients, tossing until blended.

Gourmet Tomato Sauce

Makes 2¼ cups

1 package (1½ ounces) spaghetti sauce mix with imported mushrooms
1 can (6 ounces) tomato paste
2 cups water
3 tablespoons olive or salad oil
¼ cup red wine

1. Blend spaghetti sauce mix, tomato paste, water and olive oil in a saucepan; bring to a boil.
2. Reduce heat and simmer, uncovered, 25 minutes.
3. Add wine; simmer a few minutes more.

Salmon-Spinach Turnovers

Makes 6 turnovers

1 can (7¾ ounces) salmon, drained and flaked
½ cup cooked spinach, well drained
¼ cup minced onion
1 egg, beaten
1 package (10 ounces) frozen patty shells, thawed
1 package (3 ounces) cream cheese, cut in thin slices
lemon juice

1. Combine salmon, spinach and onion; set aside.
2. Roll each patty shell into a 7-inch circle, trimming edges if necessary.
3. Place ⅙ of cream cheese slices over half of each circle; top with ⅙ of salmon-spinach-onion mixture.
4. Squeeze a few drops lemon juice over all.
5. Moisten edges of pastry with water; fold pastry over to form a half-circle, sealing edges well with a fork.
6. Brush top with beaten egg.
7. Repeat process for all turnovers.
8. Bake in preheated 400° F. oven 18 to 20 minutes, or until golden brown.

MAINDISH FARE												FISH

Sweet & Sour Shrimp in the Shell
Serves 4 to 6

1 fresh pineapple
1 medium onion, quartered
1 cup diagonally sliced celery
2 tablespoons salad oil
⅔ cup firmly packed brown sugar
2 tablespoons cornstarch
½ teaspoon salt
⅛ teaspoon ginger
⅓ cup vinegar
3 tablespoons soy sauce
1 can (6 ounces) pineapple juice
1¼ cups water
1 pound cooked and cleaned fresh shrimp or canned shrimp
1 green pepper, cut into 1-inch pieces
hot cooked rice

1. Cut top from pineapple; set aside.
2. Cut out pineapple with a sharp knife, leaving ½-inch shell; set shell aside.
3. Cut fresh pineapple into cubes to make 2 cups; set aside.
4. Sauté onion and celery in hot oil; set aside.
5. Combine brown sugar, cornstarch, salt and ginger; dissolve in vinegar and soy sauce.
6. Add vinegar mixture, pineapple juice and water to sautéed onion and celery; cook, stirring constantly, until thickened and clear.
7. Add reserved pineapple, shrimp and green pepper; cover and continue cooking 5 minutes.
8. Spoon mixture into the pineapple shell; cover with pineapple top.
9. Serve with a side dish of hot cooked rice.

Rock Lobster Wellington
Serves 6

2 pounds frozen South African rock lobster tails
boiling salted water
2 eggs, well beaten
1 cup minced celery
1 large onion, chopped
¼ cup butter
4 cups soft bread crumbs
1 teaspoon grated lemon rind
2 tablespoons lemon juice
salt to taste
pepper to taste
1 package pie crust mix
milk
2 cups tomato or mushroom sauce

1. Parboil frozen rock lobster tails by dropping into boiling salted water; when water reboils, drain immediately and drench with cold water.
2. Remove meat from shells (reserve some of the shells for filling with hot vegetables such as peas, carrots, green beans, etc., to be served with hot Wellington). Chop rock lobster meat; mix with eggs.
3. Sauté celery and onion in butter until tender.
4. Fold sautéed vegetables (with drippings), bread crumbs, lemon rind, lemon juice, salt and pepper into rock lobster mixture.
5. Prepare pie crust according to package directions; roll out ¾ of dough into 10 × 14-inch rectangle on lightly floured board.
6. Shape rock lobster mixture on pie crust into a long narrow loaf.
7. Moisten edges of pie crust with water; fold crust around loaf of rock lobster mixture, enclosing it completely.

Salmon-Filled Crêpes
Serves 6

- 6 tablespoons butter or margarine
- 2½ cups (½ pound) sliced mushrooms
- 1 cup diced celery
- ⅓ cup chopped onion
- ⅓ cup all-purpose flour
- 2 chicken bouillon cubes
- 1½ cups boiling water
- 1 teaspoon original Worcestershire sauce
- 1 teaspoon lemon juice
- 1 can (1 pound) salmon, drained and flaked
- 1 cup dairy sour cream
- 2 tablespoons chopped parsley
- 12 Crêpes
- 1 cup shredded Swiss cheese
- 6 lemon wedges (optional)

1. Melt butter in a skillet; add mushrooms and sauté 2 minutes.
2. Add celery and onion; sauté 3 minutes.
3. Blend in flour; cook and stir over low heat 1 minute.
4. Dissolve bouillon cubes in boiling water; add to mushroom mixture with Worcestershire sauce and lemon juice.
5. Cook and stir over low heat until mixture thickens, about 2 minutes.
6. Blend in salmon, sour cream and parsley; heat just until hot.
7. Spoon ¼ cup of mixture on each crêpe; roll up and place, seam-side down, in a buttered 12 × 7½ × 2-inch baking pan.
8. Spoon remaining filling over crêpes; sprinkle cheese over all.
9. Bake in a preheated 350° F. oven 20 minutes, or until hot and cheese is melted.
10. If desired, place under a preheated hot broiler 2 minutes to brown cheese.
11. Serve with lemon wedges if desired.

Crêpes
Makes 12

- 2 eggs
- ⅔ cup milk
- 1 tablespoon butter or margarine, melted
- ½ cup all-purpose flour
- ¼ teaspoon salt
- corn oil

1. Beat eggs thoroughly in a medium-size mixing bowl.
2. Stir in milk and butter; blend in flour and salt just until smooth.
3. Lightly brush a 5-inch crêpe pan with oil; heat over medium heat.
4. Add 2 measuring tablespoons of batter; tilt pan so batter covers entire bottom.
5. Cook 2 minutes on each side, or until golden; repeat.
6. Pile crêpes on top of each other on a plate. (Crêpes may be freezer-wrapped and stored in freezer until needed.)

(Preceding recipe, steps continued:)

8. Place loaf, seam-side down, on greased cookie sheet; brush with milk.
9. Roll out remaining pie crust; cut into strips and flowers, using a sharp knife and cookie cutters.
10. Place decorations on loaf; brush again with milk.
11. Bake in preheated 400° F. oven 30 to 35 minutes, or until crust is golden brown.
12. Serve hot with tomato or mushroom sauce and with vegetable-filled shells.

Baked Snapper with Sour Cream Stuffing

Serves 6

- 1 cleaned, scaled fresh snapper with head and tail attached, weighing 3 to 4 pounds
- 1 teaspoon salt
- ¾ cup celery, chopped
- ½ cup minced onion
- ¼ cup melted butter or margarine
- 4 cups dry bread crumbs
- ½ cup dairy sour cream
- ¼ cup peeled lemon or lime, diced finely
- 2 tablespoons lemon or lime rind, grated
- 1 teaspoon paprika
- 1 teaspoon pepper
- cooking oil

1. Wash fish inside and out in cool running water; rinse and dry completely.
2. Sprinkle with ½ teaspoon salt; set aside.
3. Sauté celery and onion in butter, cooking until slightly wilted and tender; remove from heat.
4. Add remaining ½ teaspoon salt with remaining ingredients except oil, mixing thoroughly.
5. Stuff fish cavity loosely with stuffing; close opening with metal skewers, using string to tie tightly.
6. Place fish in a greased baking dish that will accommodate both head and tail; brush with cooking oil.
7. Bake in preheated 350° F. oven for 30 to 40 minutes, or until meat flakes easily, making sure to baste with oil every 7 to 8 minutes.
8. Remove skewers and serve in same pan.

Tuna Dutch Baby with Tuna-Vegetable Filling

Serves 4

- 2 eggs
- ½ cup unsifted flour
- ½ cup milk
- ¼ teaspoon salt
- 1 tablespoon butter or margarine
- Tuna-Vegetable Filling

1. Combine eggs, flour, milk and salt in a small bowl; beat with an electric mixer or rotary beater until smooth.
2. Heat a 10-inch ovenproof skillet in a 450° F. oven 3 minutes, or until skillet is very hot.
3. Remove skillet from oven; drop butter in skillet, allowing butter to melt.
4. Immediately add batter; return skillet to 450° F. oven and bake 12 minutes.
5. Reduce heat to 350° F.; continue baking 10 to 15 minutes longer, until batter puffs and is golden brown.
6. Remove Dutch pancake to heated serving platter; fill with Tuna-Vegetable Filling.

Tuna-Vegetable Filling

3 tablespoons butter or margarine
¾ cup diced red or green peppers
1 can (4 ounces) sliced mushrooms, drained
2 tablespoons flour
1½ cups milk
1 cup cooked peas
1 can (6½ or 7 ounces) tuna, drained and flaked
½ teaspoon salt
dash of pepper
¼ teaspoon ground nutmeg

1. Melt 1 tablespoon butter in a medium-size saucepan.
2. Sauté peppers and mushrooms in butter until peppers are crisp-tender; remove and set aside.
3. In the same saucepan, melt remaining butter; stir in flour and milk and cook, stirring constantly, until mixture boils and thickens.
4. Add cooked peppers and mushrooms, peas, tuna, salt, pepper and nutmeg; mix well.
5. Cook mixture over low heat until heated through.

Moussaka di Mare

Serves 6

1 large eggplant, sliced ½-inch thick
salt
corn oil
6 tablespoons butter or margarine
1 large onion, chopped (1 cup)
1 clove garlic, minced
1 can (1 pound) tomatoes, drained
2 cans (6½ or 7 ounces each) tuna, drained of excess liquid
3 tablespoons tomato paste
⅛ teaspoon ground cinnamon
⅛ teaspoon pepper
¼ cup flour
2 cups milk
3 eggs, beaten
⅔ cup grated Parmesan cheese

1. Sprinkle eggplant slices with salt; let stand 15 minutes.
2. Pat slices dry; place on oiled baking sheet.
3. Melt 2 tablespoons butter in a medium-size skillet; add oil.
4. Brush eggplant with half the oil mixture.
5. Bake in preheated 350° F. oven 10 minutes; remove and set aside.
6. Sauté onion and garlic in the same skillet until tender.
7. Add tomatoes, tuna, tomato paste, cinnamon, ¼ teaspoon salt and pepper; mix well.
8. Heat mixture 3 minutes, stirring occasionally.
9. Melt remaining butter in saucepan; stir in flour and ¼ teaspoon salt. Cook 1 minute.
10. Gradually add milk; stir until mixture boils and thickens.
11. Gradually pour hot sauce into eggs, stirring constantly; stir in cheese.
12. Arrange half the eggplant slices in a shallow 2-quart baking dish; cover with tuna mixture.
13. Top with remaining eggplant slices; pour cheese sauce over all.
14. Bake in preheated 350° F. oven 40 minutes, until golden brown.

MAINDISH FARE   BEEF

Beef Roll-Ups with Sausage

Serves 4

- ¼ pound bulk pork sausage
- ½ cup chopped apple
- ¼ cup minced onion
- 1 cup toasted small bread cubes
- 1 tablespoon chopped parsley
- 1 pound thinly sliced round steak (¼-inch thick)
- 2 tablespoons shortening
- 1 can (10½ ounces) mushroom gravy
- generous dash of crushed rosemary

1. Cook sausage with apple and onion in a saucepan until meat is browned; add bread cubes and parsley.
2. Cut steak into 4 pieces; pound with meat hammer or edge of heavy saucer.
3. Place about ⅓ cup stuffing near center of each piece of meat.
4. Starting at narrow end, roll up; tuck in ends and fasten with toothpicks or skewers.
5. Brown roll-ups in shortening in a skillet; pour off fat.
6. Add remaining ingredients; cover and cook over low heat 1¼ hours, or until tender, stirring often.

Peachy Beef Pinwheel

Serves 8

- 1 can (16 ounces) sliced cling peaches
- 2 pounds ground beef
- 1½ cups soft bread crumbs
- 2 eggs
- 1 small onion, finely chopped
- 2 teaspoons dill weed
- 2 teaspoons salt
- ¼ teaspoon pepper
- 1 cup cooked rice
- 1 tablespoon snipped parsley
- ¼ teaspoon nutmeg

1. Drain peaches, reserving syrup; cut slices in half crosswise.
2. Combine beef, bread crumbs, eggs, onion, ⅓ cup reserved syrup, dill weed, salt and pepper.
3. Combine rice, parsley and 1 tablespoon reserved syrup.
4. Pat out meat mixture on waxed paper into a 14 x 10-inch rectangle, ½- to ¾-inch thick.
5. Spread rice mixture evenly over meat.
6. Stir nutmeg into peaches; place over meat, distributing evenly.
7. Roll up meat mixture, jelly-roll fashion, from short side of rectangle to enclose peaches and form a pinwheel loaf.
8. Press meat over filling at both ends of loaf; place, seam-side down, on rack in roasting pan.
9. Bake in preheated 350° F. oven 1 hour.
10. Brush with reserved peach juice; continue baking 15 minutes.
11. Let stand 10 minutes before slicing.

Corn-Stuffed Beef Birds

Serves 5 to 6

- ¼ cup flour
- 1¾ teaspoons salt
- ½ teaspoon pepper
- 1 beef round steak, cut ½-inch thick
- 1 can (12 ounces) whole kernel corn
- ¾ cup cracker crumbs
- 2 tablespoons chopped onion
- 1 tablespoon green pepper
- ¼ teaspoon basil
- 2 tablespoons lard or drippings
- ¼ cup water

1. Mix together flour, 1½ teaspoons salt and ¼ teaspoon pepper; pound seasoned flour into steak.
2. Cut steak into 5 to 6 servings.
3. Mix together corn, cracker crumbs, onion, green pepper, basil and remaining salt and pepper.
4. Place ⅓ cup corn mixture on each piece of steak; roll up jelly-roll fashion and fasten with wooden picks or skewers.
5. Brown meat slowly in lard; add water, cover tightly and cook slowly 1½ hours, or until meat is tender. (Thicken cooking liquid for gravy if desired.)

Stuffed Beef Rolls with Sherried Asparagus Sauce

Serves 4

- 1 tablespoon butter or margarine
- ⅓ cup minced onion
- ⅓ cup minced celery
- 1 clove garlic, minced
- 1½ cups soft bread crumbs
- 3 tablespoons grated Parmesan cheese
- 1 tablespoon chopped parsley
- 1 teaspoon marjoram
- ¼ teaspoon sage
- ⅛ teaspoon pepper
- 4 beef top round butterfly steaks
- 2 tablespoons vegetable shortening
- 1 can (10¾ ounces) condensed cream of asparagus soup, undiluted
- ¼ cup milk
- 1 package (8 ounces) frozen asparagus cuts and tips
- 2 tablespoons dry sherry (optional)

1. Melt butter in a small skillet.
2. Add onion, celery and garlic; sauté until onion is transparent.
3. Remove from heat; place onion mixture in a medium-size bowl.
4. Add bread crumbs, cheese, parsley, marjoram, sage and pepper to bowl; stir with a fork until well combined.
5. Divide mixture into 4 portions; place 1 portion on each steak.
6. Roll steak, jelly-roll fashion; secure ends with short skewers, wooden toothpicks, or tie with string.
7. Melt shortening in a medium-size skillet; brown meat rolls well.
8. Combine soup, milk and asparagus; pour into skillet around meat.
9. Cover and simmer 25 to 30 minutes, or until meat is tender.
10. Add sherry before serving; serve meat with asparagus sauce spooned over top.

Milano Beef Torte

Serves 6

Crêpes (page 17)
1½ pounds ground beef
1 onion, chopped
1 teaspoon Italian seasoning
1 teaspoon salt
1 package (1½ ounces) spaghetti sauce mix

1 can (15 ounces) tomato sauce
1 package (10 ounces) frozen chopped spinach, defrosted and well drained
1 cup shredded mozzarella cheese
2 tablespoons grated Parmesan cheese

1. Prepare Crêpes; set aside.
2. Cook beef and onion in a large frying pan; pour off drippings.
3. Sprinkle Italian seasoning and ½ teaspoon salt over meat.
4. Combine spaghetti sauce mix with tomato sauce; reserving ¼ cup mixture, stir remaining sauce mixture into meat.
5. Combine spinach, ½ cup mozzarella cheese, Parmesan cheese and remaining salt.
6. To assemble torte, place ingredients in layers in 8-inch springform pan or 9-inch pie plate in the following order: 2 crêpes, half the meat mixture, crêpe, spinach mixture, crêpe, remainder of meat mixture and crêpe.
7. Cover torte loosely with foil; bake in preheated 350° F. oven 40 minutes.
8. Remove foil; spread reserved sauce on top and sprinkle with remaining mozzarella cheese.
9. Continue baking 5 minutes; let torte stand 5 minutes before cutting into wedges.

Beef Wellington

Serves 8

3½ pounds beef tenderloin
Pastry
1 egg, beaten
8 ounces liver sausage or liver pâté

1. Place tenderloin on rack in an open roasting pan. (Do not add water. Do not cover.)
2. Roast in preheated 425° F. oven, allowing a total (depending on size of roast) of 20 to 25 minutes for rare, 25 to 30 minutes for medium.
3. Remove roast from oven; let stand 30 minutes.
4. Prepare pastry; roll into an 18 × 14-inch rectangle, ¼-inch thick.
5. Spread pâté over surface of pastry; place tenderloin lengthwise, top down, in the middle of pastry.
6. Bring long side of pastry up to overlap on bottom of tenderloin; brush with egg to seal.
7. Trim ends of pastry and fold over; brush with egg to seal.
8. Transfer pastry-wrapped meat, seam-side down, to baking sheet; cut decorative shapes from pastry trimmings, arrange on top and brush top and sides with egg.
9. If desired, check internal temperature by inserting roast meat thermometer, being sure bulb is centered in thickest part and does not rest in fat.
10. Bake in preheated 425° F. oven 30 minutes; let stand 10 minutes before carving.

Pastry for Beef Wellington

3 cups all-purpose flour
½ teaspoon salt
¾ cup lard
½ to ¾ cup cold water

1. Sift together flour and salt.
2. Cut in lard to form fine even crumbs.
3. Add water, 1 tablespoon at a time, until dough just holds together.
4. Shape into a ball; roll out on lightly floured board or pastry cloth.

Burger Turnovers

Serves 6

1 medium onion, minced
1 tablespoon butter or margarine
1 pound ground beef or veal
3 cups diced cooked potatoes
1½ teaspoons salt
¼ teaspoon pepper
⅛ teaspoon garlic salt
pastry for double crust 9-inch pie

1. Sauté onion in butter in a skillet; cook until tender.
2. Add meat; cook until meat loses red color, breaking up meat with a fork to keep it crumbly.
3. Stir in potatoes, salt, pepper and garlic salt; cook 1 to 2 minutes.
4. Roll pastry on lightly floured board to ⅛-inch thickness; cut into circles 4 inches in diameter.
5. Place 1 heaping tablespoon meat mixture on each round; fold over, pressing edges of pastry together with tines of a fork.
6. Place turnovers on a baking sheet; bake in preheated 450° F. oven 12 minutes, or until golden.

Olive's Cornish Pasties

Makes 5 pasties

4 cups all-purpose flour
salt
1 teaspoon baking powder
1¾ cups lard
1 egg
1 tablespoon vinegar
½ cup water
6 medium potatoes, diced
2 medium onions, chopped
1 pound chuck roast, cut in ½-inch cubes
pepper to taste

1. Sift together flour, 1 teaspoon salt and baking powder; cut in lard.
2. Add egg, vinegar and water to form dough; mix briefly and refrigerate while preparing filling.
3. Toss together potatoes, onions and meat; season with salt and pepper to taste.
4. Roll out dough into five 8-inch circles; divide filling on half of each circle.
5. Moisten edge of dough with water; fold over and seal tightly by pressing edges with fork. Pierce top.
6. Place pasties on a cookie sheet; bake in preheated 400° F. oven 15 minutes.
7. Reduce heat to 350° F.; bake 45 minutes longer.

MAINDISH FARE — BEEF

Cannelloni

Serves 8

4 eggs
1 cup milk
1 cup unsifted all-purpose flour
½ teaspoon salt
¼ cup olive oil
1 pound ground chuck
1 onion, chopped
2 packages (10 ounces each) frozen chopped spinach, thawed and squeezed dry

1 egg
½ cup tomato purée
½ teaspoon oregano
2 teaspoons Angostura aromatic bitters
½ cup fine dry bread crumbs
¼ cup melted butter or margarine
1 cup (4 ounces) shredded mozzarella cheese
½ cup grated Parmesan cheese

1. Beat together eggs, milk, flour and salt in a bowl until smooth; let stand 1 hour.
2. Spoon 2 tablespoons batter into a lightly buttered preheated 8-inch skillet or crêpe pan; rotate pan so bottom is evenly covered with dough.
3. Brown crêpes on both sides; stack.
4. Heat oil in a skillet; sauté beef and onion until beef is brown and crumbly.
5. Drain excess fat.
6. Stir in spinach, egg, tomato purée, oregano, Angostura and crumbs; stir until well blended.
7. Use mixture to fill crêpes; roll up crêpes and place side by side in a single layer in a buttered shallow baking pan.
8. Mix butter and cheeses; sprinkle mixture over crêpes.
9. Bake in preheated 400° F. oven 15 to 20 minutes, or until crusty brown and piping hot.

Beef Dolmades

Serves 8

1 large head cabbage to provide 8 large leaves
boiling water
2 pounds ground beef
½ cup uncooked rice
2 eggs, beaten
1 large onion, finely cut

⅛ teaspoon garlic powder
2 teaspoons salt
½ teaspoon cracked pepper
¼ teaspoon rosemary
½ teaspoon celery salt
Beef Dolmades Sauce

1. Core a large head of cabbage; remove 8 leaves.
2. Trim off thick part of leaves and cover with boiling water; let stand 5 minutes.
3. Meanwhile, mix together ground beef, rice, eggs, onion and seasonings.
4. Remove leaves from water; drain.
5. Place equal portions of mixture on each of 8 leaves; roll up.
6. Place each dolmade, seam-side down, in a heavy skillet or casserole; pour on Beef Dolmades Sauce.

7. Cover and bake in preheated 375° F. oven 1 hour.
8. Remove cover; bake ½ hour longer, basting often with sauce during cooking.

Beef Dolmades Sauce

- 3 cans (8 ounces each) tomato sauce
- 1 cup beef bouillon or broth
- 1 small green pepper, finely cut
- ⅓ cup sugar
- ¼ teaspoon rosemary
- 1 large onion, finely cut
- 3 to 4 celery stalks, minced
- 1 tablespoon parsley flakes
- 1 teaspoon salt
- ½ teaspoon cracked pepper

Mix thoroughly; pour over dolmades.

Dilled Cabbage Rolls

Serves 10 to 12

- 1 head (3 pounds) green cabbage, cored
- boiling water
- 1 pound ground lean pork
- 1 pound ground lean beef, divided
- 1½ cups cooked rice
- ⅔ cup finely chopped onions, divided
- 4 tablespoons original Worcestershire sauce, divided
- 1 tablespoon chopped parsley
- 1¼ teaspoons salt, divided
- ¼ teaspoon Tabasco sauce
- 1 can (1 pound) tomatoes, broken up
- 1 can (8 ounces) tomato sauce
- 1 teaspoon dill seed
- ½ teaspoon sugar

1. Place cabbage in a large saucepot filled with boiling water; cover and cook until leaves separate from head, removing them as this occurs.
2. Drain leaves.
3. Trim thick center vein from cabbage leaves, being careful not to tear leaves; set leaves aside.
4. Combine pork, half the beef, rice, ⅓ cup onion, 2 tablespoons Worcestershire sauce, parsley, 1 teaspoon salt and Tabasco in a mixing bowl; mix well, but do not overmix.
5. Place a heaping tablespoon of filling in the center of each cabbage leaf; fold two sides over filling and roll up. Fasten with toothpicks, if needed.
6. Place leftover cabbage in a large saucepot; arrange stuffed cabbage over leaves, seam-side down.
7. Brown remaining beef in a skillet, stirring often.
8. Combine browned meat with tomatoes, tomato sauce, dill, sugar and remaining onion, Worcestershire sauce and salt; mix well.
9. Pour meat sauce over stuffed cabbage; bring to a boil.
10. Reduce heat and simmer, covered, 2 to 2½ hours.

Beef & Barley Cabbage Rolls

Serves 6

½ cup uncooked barley
2 cups water
2 teaspoons salt
1 head green cabbage (about 2½ pounds)
1 pound lean ground beef
½ cup minced onion
½ cup minced parsley
1 egg, lightly beaten
⅔ cup evaporated milk
¼ teaspoon pepper
½ teaspoon marjoram
⅛ teaspoon garlic salt (optional)
1 tablespoon butter

1. Place barley in a sieve; rinse thoroughly with cold water.
2. Place barley in a saucepan with 2 cups water and 1 teaspoon salt; simmer gently 45 minutes, or until barley is tender and water has evaporated.
3. Remove from heat; cool.
4. Cut out core of cabbage; let cold water run into opening to loosen leaves.
5. Remove 12 leaves from head, keeping them whole.
6. Place leaves in covered kettle with ½ inch water; steam 5 minutes to wilt.
7. Remove carefully; drain well.
8. Mix together cooled barley, meat, onion, parsley, egg, evaporated milk, remaining teaspoon salt, pepper, marjoram and garlic salt, if desired.
9. Divide into 12 portions; place filling on stem end of cabbage leaves and roll tightly.
10. Melt butter in a large skillet; place cabbage rolls in skillet and brown lightly 25 to 30 minutes.
11. Remove to hot serving platter.

Swedish Cabbage Rolls

Serves 6

6 large cabbage leaves
½ pound lean ground beef
½ cup cooked rice
1 can (8½ ounces) whole kernel golden corn, drained, liquid reserved
2 tablespoons minced onion
½ cup cubed pasteurized process cheese spread
1 egg, beaten
¼ teaspoon salt
dash of pepper
½ teaspoon original Worcestershire sauce
1 can (8 ounces) tomato sauce

1. Steam cabbage leaves 3 minutes in a covered pan; drain and set aside.
2. Brown ground beef in a skillet; drain excess fat.
3. Add rice, corn, onion, cheese, egg, salt, pepper and Worcestershire sauce to meat in skillet.
4. Place ½ cup meat mixture on each reserved cabbage leaf; fold in sides and roll up ends, securing with a toothpick.
5. Place rolls, folded-side up, in a 10-inch skillet.
6. Combine tomato sauce and reserved corn liquid; pour over cabbage rolls, cover and simmer 30 minutes.

BEEF MAINDISH FARE

Lasagna Roll-Ups

Serves 4

1 pound ground beef
2 cloves garlic, crushed
2 teaspoons seasoned salt
½ teaspoon seasoned pepper
1 can (6 ounces) tomato paste
1 package (1½ ounces) spaghetti sauce mix with imported mushrooms
1 can (1 pound 12 ounces) tomatoes, cut up
8 lasagna noodles, cooked and drained
8 ounces ricotta cheese
8 ounces mozzarella cheese, grated
½ cup grated Parmesan cheese

1. Brown beef in a Dutch oven; drain fat.
2. Add garlic, seasoned salt, seasoned pepper, tomato paste, spaghetti mix and tomatoes; stir thoroughly.
3. Bring mixture to a boil; reduce heat, cover and simmer 30 minutes, stirring occasionally.
4. Lay two noodles side by side on wax paper; spread with ¼ of the ricotta.
5. Then spread with ½ cup of meat mixture and ¼ of mozzarella and Parmesan cheeses.
6. Roll up noodles; place, seam-side down, in 12 × 8 × 2-inch baking dish.
7. Prepare remaining 3 roll-ups.
8. Top roll-ups with remaining meat sauce; bake, uncovered, in preheated 350° F. oven 20 to 30 minutes, or until heated.

Machaca de Huevos

Makes 6 servings or 8 burritos

salad oil
1½ pounds flank steak
seasoned salt
seasoned pepper
2 cups water
4 onions, halved and sliced
1 green bell pepper, diced
2 tomatoes, diced
1 dozen eggs, beaten
2 cups grated Cheddar cheese
8 flour tortillas (optional)

1. Heat oil in a large skillet.
2. Season flank steak liberally with seasoned salt and seasoned pepper; brown meat on both sides.
3. Add water; bring to a boil, reduce heat and simmer, covered, 2 hours, or until tender. (Add more water during cooking if necessary.)
4. When meat is tender, shred into medium-size pieces.
5. Heat 2 to 3 tablespoons oil in a large skillet; quickly sauté onions, green pepper and tomatoes.
6. Add meat, eggs and cheese; continue cooking as for scrambled eggs.
7. Serve as an entrée, or use as burrito filling. To make burritos, place about 1 cup filling in center of flour tortilla, fold sides in and roll up.

Blanketed Beef Loaf

Serves 8

2 pounds ground beef
1½ cups soft bread crumbs
1 egg
¼ cup plus 2 tablespoons catsup
⅓ cup salad olives
1 tablespoon prepared mustard
1 teaspoon salt
½ teaspoon rubbed sage
⅛ teaspoon pepper
pastry for double-crust pie

1. Combine beef, bread crumbs, egg, catsup, olives, mustard, salt, sage and pepper lightly but thoroughly.
2. Place mixture in a 9 × 5-inch loaf pan, pressing lightly to fill evenly; chill in refrigerator while preparing pastry.
3. Turn loaf out of pan onto rack in roasting pan; spread top with 2 tablespoons catsup.
4. Roll out pastry on a lightly floured board into a 10 × 15-inch rectangle, ⅛- to ¼-inch thick; cut into 8 strips, 1 inch wide and 10 inches long.
5. Place pastry strips crosswise over loaf to cover top and sides, pressing them to loaf. (Leave ends open.)
6. Cut 8 strips from remaining pastry; twist and use to decorate loaf.
7. Bake in preheated 375° F. oven 50 minutes, or until meat loaf is done and pastry lightly browned.
8. Let stand 10 minutes before slicing.

Carrie's Cabbage Meat Loaf

Serves 6 to 8

1 medium-size cabbage
boiling water
1½ pounds lean ground beef
2 teaspoons salt
1¼ teaspoons pepper
1½ tablespoons minced onion
¾ cup flour
½ teaspoon celery seeds
½ cup milk
2 tablespoons minced parsley
2 eggs
1 can (8 ounces) tomato sauce
1 tablespoon sugar
1 teaspoon original Worcestershire sauce
dairy sour cream (optional)

1. Cut cabbage in quarters; remove core.
2. Cover with boiling water; cook 10 minutes.
3. Drain; separate leaves.
4. Combine meat, salt, pepper, onion, flour, celery seeds, milk, parsley and eggs.
5. Grease a 9 × 5-inch loaf pan; fill alternately with layers of meat and cabbage leaves, beginning and ending with meat.
6. Combine tomato sauce, sugar and Worcestershire sauce; pour over top.
7. Bake in preheated 375° F. oven 1 hour.
8. Serve with dollop of sour cream if desired.

Carrot-Stuffed Meat Loaf

Serves 6

5 medium carrots, peeled and chopped (1¼ cups)
boiling water
¾ cup wheat germ
½ cup chopped onion
1 teaspoon grated orange peel
½ cup fresh orange juice
¼ teaspoon thyme leaves, crushed
2¼ teaspoons original Worcestershire sauce
2 eggs, beaten
1¼ pounds ground beef
¼ cup orange marmalade

1. Parboil carrots in 1 inch boiling water for 5 minutes; drain and set aside to cool.
2. Combine wheat germ, onion, orange peel, orange juice, thyme, Worcestershire sauce and eggs in a large bowl.
3. Add ¼ cup wheat germ mixture to cooled carrots; mix well and set aside.
4. Add beef to remaining wheat germ mixture; mix well.
5. Spoon ⅔ meat mixture into an ungreased 8½ × 4½ × 2½-inch loaf pan; make a well running lengthwise down the center.
6. Spoon carrot mixture into well; cover with remaining meat mixture. Pat down firmly.
7. Bake in preheated 350° F. oven until meat is firm, about 1¼ hours.
8. Heat broiler to hot.
9. Spread marmalade on top of meat loaf; broil until marmalade is bubbling and glazed, about 5 minutes.
10. Let meat stand in pan 10 minutes before turning out on serving dish.

Meat Loaf Roll-Up, American Style

Serves 6 to 8

1½ cups cracked wheat bread, cubed
1 cup whole berry cranberry sauce
½ cup chopped onion
½ cup minced celery with leaves
2 eggs
1½ pounds ground beef or veal
2 tablespoons minced parsley
1 teaspoon salt
¼ cup milk

1. Combine bread cubes, ½ cup cranberry sauce, ¼ cup onion, ¼ cup celery and 1 beaten egg; blend well. Set aside.
2. In a separate bowl, combine beef with remaining onion, celery and egg; add parsley, salt and milk.
3. On waxed paper, pat out meat mixture to form a 12 × 10-inch rectangle.
4. Spoon bread mixture on top of meat to cover; roll up, using waxed paper to help, starting from narrow end.
5. Place roll in a shallow baking pan; bake in preheated 350° F. oven 1¼ hours.
6. Spoon remaining cranberry sauce over all; bake 15 minutes longer.
7. Slice to serve.

MAINDISH FARE   BEEF

Italian Tortilla Stacks

Serves 8 to 10

1½ pounds ground beef
1 package (1⅝ ounces) lasagna sauce mix
1 teaspoon seasoned salt
1 can (1 pound) tomatoes, cut up
1 can (8 ounces) tomato sauce
½ cup water
1 can (4 ounces) diced green chilies
1 pound ricotta cheese
2 eggs
8 fresh corn tortillas
1 pound Monterey Jack cheese, grated

1. Brown beef in a large skillet until crumbly; drain fat.
2. Add sauce mix, seasoned salt, tomatoes, tomato sauce, water and green chilies; blend thoroughly.
3. Simmer on low for 10 minutes.
4. Meanwhile, combine ricotta and eggs in small bowl; blend thoroughly.
5. Spread cheese mixture evenly on each tortilla.
6. Spread 1 cup meat sauce in 12 × 8 × 2-inch baking dish.
7. Place two cheese-topped tortillas side by side in baking dish; spread ⅓ cup of meat-sauce mixture and ⅓ cup grated cheese over each.
8. Repeat until each stack contains 4 tortillas, layered with meat sauce and cheese.
9. Bake in preheated 350° F. oven 30 minutes; let stand 5 minutes before cutting into pie-shaped wedges.

NOTE: Great dish to prepare ahead! Allow at least 45 minutes to reheat after refrigerating dish.

Angostura Minute Steaks

Serves 6

1 egg
1 tablespoon Angostura aromatic bitters
12 beef cube steaks, seasoned with salt and pepper
1½ cups cornflake crumbs
⅓ cup grated Parmesan cheese
¼ cup corn oil
1 can (8 ounces) tomato sauce

1. Beat together egg and Angostura in a bowl.
2. Dip steaks in egg mixture; coat well.
3. Mix crumbs and cheese in separate bowl.
4. Dip egg-coated steaks into crumb mixture, pressing firmly to make crumbs adhere.
5. Place steaks, side by side, in a shallow baking pan; drizzle steaks with oil.
6. Bake in preheated 350° F. oven 20 to 25 minutes, or until richly browned.
7. Spoon tomato sauce evenly over steaks; bake 5 minutes longer.

NOTE: Serve with spaghetti dusted with Parmesan cheese and zucchini slices braised with chopped fresh tomatoes and onions.

Rouladen

Serves 6

- 1½ pounds round steak, ½-inch thick
- 6 teaspoons Dijon-style mustard
- 6 thin slices ham, fully cooked
- 3 dill pickles, split lengthwise
- ¼ cup vegetable shortening
- 2 cups tomato juice
- ½ cup chopped onion
- ½ cup chopped celery
- 1 teaspoon instant beef-flavored bouillon
- 2 tablespoons cornstarch
- ¼ cup water
- 1 cup dairy sour cream

1. Cut steak into 6 rectangular pieces; pound to ¼-inch thick.
2. Spread each piece with 1 teaspoon mustard, top with ham, and place pickle at narrow end.
3. Roll up, jelly-roll fashion; secure with toothpicks or tie with string.
4. Melt shortening in a skillet; brown meat rolls on all sides.
5. Add tomato juice, onion, celery and bouillon; bring to a boil.
6. Reduce heat; simmer, covered, 2 hours.
7. Remove meat to a serving dish; set aside and keep warm.
8. Blend cornstarch and water; stir cornstarch mixture slowly into the sauce in the skillet.
9. Heat sauce to a boil, stirring constantly; boil 1 minute.
10. Remove from heat; slowly add the sour cream.
11. Serve as a gravy with Rouladen.

Flank Steak, Creole Style

Serves 6

- 1 large beef flank steak, weighing about 2 pounds
- ½ pound pork sausage
- 1 cup moist bread crumbs
- 2 tablespoons chopped parsley
- 2 tablespoons lard
- 2 teaspoons salt
- ½ cup chopped onions
- 2 bay leaves
- 1 can (16 ounces) tomatoes
- ½ cup chopped green pepper (optional)
- 1 cup water
- 3 tablespoons flour

1. Pound or lightly score flank steak on both sides.
2. Combine sausage, bread crumbs and parsley; mix well.
3. Spread the sausage mixture on the flank steak; roll up in a jelly roll.
4. Tie steak with string; brown in lard.
5. Pour off drippings.
6. Add salt, onions, bay leaves, tomatoes and green pepper; cover and cook slowly 1½ to 2 hours, or until tender.
7. Remove steak and bay leaves; pour off excess fat.
8. Add water and flour to cooking liquid; cook until thickened for gravy.

MAINDISH FARE   BEEF

Steak Roll-Ups
Serves 6

- 2 tablespoons oil, divided
- ½ cup minced carrots
- 2 tablespoons minced onion
- 2 tablespoons minced green pepper
- 1½ cups chopped mushrooms
- 1¼ teaspoons salt, divided
- 2 tablespoons original Worcestershire sauce, divided
- 6 individual (2 pounds) beef cubed steaks or chuck top blade steaks
- 3 tablespoons water
- 1 tablespoon catsup

1. Heat 1 tablespoon oil in a large skillet.
2. Add carrots, onion and green pepper; sauté 3 minutes.
3. Add mushrooms; sauté 3 minutes.
4. Stir in ½ teaspoon salt and 1 tablespoon Worcestershire sauce; set aside.
5. Blend remaining Worcestershire sauce with remaining salt; brush ½ teaspoon of this mixture over one side of each steak.
6. Turn steaks over; spoon about 1 tablespoon mushroom mixture on narrow side of each steak.
7. Roll steak; secure with toothpicks.
8. Repeat.
9. In the original skillet, heat remaining 1 tablespoon oil.
10. Add meat rolls; brown well on all sides, about 10 minutes.
11. Remove to serving platter.
12. Add water and catsup to skillet, stirring to loosen browned particles from bottom of pan; heat until hot.
13. Spoon over steaks and serve.

Vegetable Pie
Serves 6

- pastry for 9-inch, 2-crust pie
- 1 pound very lean ground beef
- 1 can (17 ounces) whole kernel golden corn, drained
- 1 can (8 ounces) sliced carrots, drained
- ½ cup chopped celery
- ⅓ cup chopped onion
- salt to taste
- pepper to taste

1. In unbaked pastry shell, place one-third of the uncooked beef; top with half the corn, all the carrots, half the celery, and half the onion.
2. Season to taste with salt and pepper.
3. Add another third of beef and remaining vegetables.
4. Top with remaining third of beef, salt and pepper.
5. Place top crust over pie, sealing edges; make slits in top crust to allow steam to escape.
6. Bake in preheated 450° F. oven 10 minutes.
7. Reduce heat to 350° F.; bake 50 minutes longer.

BEEF   MAINDISH FARE

Beanpot o' Gold

Serves 5

- 1 package (7½ or 8½ ounces) corn muffin mix
- ¼ cup orange marmalade
- 1 can (1 pound) pork and beans
- ½ pound wieners, cut into chunks
- ¼ cup brown sugar
- ¼ cup catsup

1. Prepare muffin mix according to package directions; pour into well-greased 9-inch ring mold.
2. Bake in preheated 375° F. oven 30 minutes.
3. Unmold ring; spread with orange marmalade.
4. Meanwhile, combine remaining ingredients and heat to serving temperature.
5. Fill center of ring with heated bean mixture.

Corn Dogs 'n Beans

Serves 8

- 1 cup pancake mix
- 2 tablespoons cornmeal
- 1 tablespoon sugar
- ⅔ cup water
- 8 frankfurters
- corn oil for deep-fat frying
- 1 can (1 pound 15 ounces) pork and beans
- ½ cup catsup
- ¼ cup brown sugar
- 1 tablespoon pickle relish

1. Combine pancake mix, cornmeal and sugar; beat in water until smooth.
2. Dip three-fourths of each frankfurter into batter, allowing excess to drain off.
3. Using a deep saucepan, fry corn dogs in hot oil at 375° F. until golden brown; drain.
4. Meanwhile, combine remaining ingredients; heat to serving temperature.
5. Serve pork and beans along with Corn Dogs.

NOTE: This is a terrific dish for teen-agers' party!

Dieter's Shepherd's Pie

Serves 4

- 1 pound ground beef
- ½ cup sliced celery
- ¼ cup chopped onion
- 1 can (10½ ounces) vegetarian vegetable soup
- ⅛ teaspoon thyme leaves, crushed
- 2 cups seasoned mashed potatoes

1. Brown beef in saucepan with celery and onion until beef is tender.
2. Stir to separate meat; pour off fat.
3. Stir in soup and thyme.
4. Pour into 1½-quart casserole; spoon potatoes around edge of casserole.
5. Bake in preheated 400° F. oven 25 minutes, or until hot.

Stuffed Lamb Chop Special

Serves 4

- ¼ cup butter or margarine
- ½ cup chopped onions
- ¼ cup chopped mushrooms
- ½ cup chopped celery
- 1 cup soft bread crumbs
- ¼ cup chopped parsley
- 2 canned pimientos, chopped
- 1 bay leaf, crumbled
- 1 teaspoon paprika
- 1 teaspoon salt
- ¼ teaspoon pepper
- 4 double rib lamb chops, cut for stuffing

1. Melt butter in a skillet.
2. Add onions, mushrooms and celery; cook until tender, stirring occasionally.
3. Add crumbs, parsley, pimientos, bay leaf, paprika, salt and pepper; mix well.
4. Fill chops with crumb mixture.
5. Place in shallow baking pan; bake in preheated 300° F. oven 1½ hours, or to desired degree of doneness.

Lamb Rolls

Serves 6

- 1 breast of lamb
- 1 cup chopped onion
- 2 large carrots, chopped
- salt to taste
- pepper to taste
- 1 tablespoon dried dill weed
- 1 cup water or lamb stock
- 2 tablespoons Dijon-style mustard
- 1 egg, lightly beaten
- 1 cup fine dry bread crumbs
- 2 tablespoons melted butter

1. Bone and roll lamb breast; secure with wooden toothpicks at 1-inch intervals.
2. Cut into 1-inch "chops."
3. Put onion and carrot in bottom of a shallow ovenproof casserole; top with lamb rolls.
4. Season to taste with salt and pepper; sprinkle dill evenly over top.
5. Pour in water.
6. Cover and bake in preheated 325° F. oven 1½ hours.
7. Remove from oven and cool.
8. Remove chops, reserving pan drippings for sauce if desired.
9. Spread mustard evenly over both sides of chops.
10. Dip chops in egg, then in crumbs.
11. Arrange chops on foil-lined broiler; drizzle melted butter over each chop.
12. Run under hot broiler, turning once to brown.
13. Serve at once.

NOTE: A tasty bite! Great for cocktails or supper!

Stuffed Breast of Lamb

Serves 4 to 6

- 1 breast of lamb, weighing 2 to 3 pounds
- 4 cups stale bread cubes
- 3 tablespoons minced onion
- ¼ cup melted butter
- ¼ cup minced celery
- 1 teaspoon sage
- 1 teaspoon salt
- ¼ teaspoon pepper
- 1 cup water

1. Have butcher cut pocket in end of lamb breast.
2. Combine remaining ingredients in a mixing bowl; mix lightly with a fork.
3. Stuff lamb breast; secure with metal skewers or tooth picks.
4. Place stuffed breast on rack in baking pan; bake in preheated 375° F. oven 2½ hours.

NOTE: If desired, breast can be basted with barbecue sauce. Deliciously inexpensive!

Lamb-Asparagus Rolls

Serves 4

- 1 can (8 ounces) tomato sauce
- 1 tablespoon butter or margarine
- ¼ cup minced onion
- ½ teaspoon garlic salt
- ¼ teaspoon salt
- 1 can (14½ ounces) asparagus spears, drained
- 4 slices cooked lamb

1. Combine tomato sauce, butter, onion, garlic salt and salt; mix well.
2. Arrange asparagus spears on lamb; roll up and fasten with toothpicks.
3. Arrange on broiler rack; top with tomato sauce mixture.
4. Broil 3 to 4 inches from source of heat 5 to 7 minutes, or until thoroughly heated.

Lamb Chops in Jackets

Serves 3

- 6 lamb chops
- 6 tablespoons butter
- ½ pound mushrooms, minced
- 1 large white onion
- 1 egg, beaten
- 2 slices ham, finely chopped
- salt to taste
- pepper to taste
- 1 pound flaky pastry

1. Trim lamb chops; sauté in 2 tablespoons butter until golden.
2. Remove chops from pan; allow to cool.
3. Add remaining butter to pan; sauté mushrooms, onion and ham.
4. Season to taste; cool.
5. Spread mushroom mixture on both sides of each chop.
6. Roll out pastry as thinly as possible; cut into 5-inch circles.
7. Wrap each circle around a chop, leaving the bone sticking out.
8. Place chops on baking sheets; brush with beaten egg.
9. Bake in preheated 450° F. oven 15 to 20 minutes.

Sweet Potato-Stuffed Pork Chops

Serves 6

- 6 pork loin rib chops, cut 1¼ inches thick
- 1 small onion, minced
- ½ cup minced celery
- 1 tablespoon butter
- 1½ cups grated raw sweet potato
- salt
- ¼ teaspoon allspice
- ¼ teaspoon sage
- 1 small apple, chopped
- ¼ cup raisins, plumped
- 2 tablespoons corn oil
- pepper

1. Cut a pocket in each chop with a small, sharp knife on the rib side parallel to the surface of each chop. (Be careful not to cut through to opposite side.)
2. Sauté onion and celery in butter until soft.
3. Stir in sweet potato, ½ teaspoon salt, allspice and sage; continue cooking 3 minutes.
4. Add apple and raisins,stirring lightly to combine; cool.
5. Fill pocket in each chop with an equal amount of stuffing.
6. Brown chops in oil.
7. Season chops on both sides with salt and pepper.
8. Place in 13 × 9 × 2-inch baking dish; cover with foil.
9. Bake in preheated 350° F. oven 45 minutes.
10. Remove foil; bake 15 minutes longer.

Texas Burritos

Serves 6

- 1½ pounds boneless pork shoulder, cut in ½-inch cubes
- 2 tablespoons vegetable oil
- water
- 1 can (8 ounces) tomato sauce
- ½ cup chopped onion
- 1 teaspoon salt
- 1 cup diced green peppers
- 1 teaspoon chili powder
- ½ teaspoon ground cumin
- 1½ teaspoons original Worcestershire sauce
- 6 flour tortillas
- ⅓ cup shredded Monterey Jack or Cheddar cheese

1. Brown pork in hot oil in a large skillet; drain fat.
2. Stir in 1½ cups water, tomato sauce, onion and salt.
3. Simmer, covered, stirring occasionally, until meat is almost tender, about 50 minutes. (Add more water if needed.)
4. Add green peppers, chili powder, cumin and Worcestershire sauce; simmer, covered, until meat and pepper are tender, 5 to 10 minutes.
5. Remove from heat.
6. Heat tortillas wrapped in foil in preheated 350° F. oven 2 minutes.
7. Spoon ½ cup meat mixture down center of each tortilla; bring opposite sides to center, overlapping slightly.
8. Place on foil-lined baking pan; sprinkle with cheese.
9. Place under hot broiler until cheese melts.

Fruit-Stuffed Pork Loin

Serves 6

1 pork loin, weighing 5 to 6 pounds
salt
pepper
¼ cup butter or margarine
2 cups onion rings
4 cups unpeeled apple slices
2 cups orange segments
1 teaspoon curry powder
1 jar (10 ounces) red currant jelly
1 can (6 ounces) frozen lemonade concentrate, thawed

1. With a sharp knife, cut along the ribs of the loin, detaching meat from bones. (Leave meat attached to bones at base of ribs.)
2. Season pork liberally with salt and pepper on all surfaces; rub seasonings into meat.
3. Heat butter in a skillet; sauté onions until golden.
4. Stir in apples, oranges, 1½ teaspoons salt and curry.
5. Stuff loin, reserving surplus.
6. Use trussing to sew loin together to contain stuffing; with a sharp knife score the surface of the pork in diamonds.
7. Place pork on a rack in a shallow baking pan; cover stuffing with a piece of foil.
8. Roast in preheated 350° F. oven 2 hours.
9. Heat currant jelly and lemonade in a saucepan until bubbly; brush glaze over meat.
10. Add remaining stuffing to cavity; roast meat 30 minutes longer, brushing with glaze every 10 minutes.
11. Serve any additional glaze as a side dish to the pork.

Sadie's Ham & 'Tater Snack

Serves 6

1 egg, beaten
¼ cup milk
½ cup fine dry bread crumbs
1 pound cooked ground ham (3 cups)
¼ cup mayonnaise
¼ teaspoon onion salt
1 package (10 ounces) frozen chopped spinach, thawed and drained
4 cups cooked mashed potatoes
½ cup shredded Swiss cheese (2 ounces)
paprika

1. Combine egg, milk and bread crumbs in a bowl.
2. Add ham; mix well.
3. Shape into an 8-inch flat round loaf on a baking sheet; bake in preheated 350° F. oven 15 minutes.
4. Combine mayonnaise, onion salt and spinach; spread spinach mixture atop ham.
5. Spread mashed potatoes over spinach to make a third layer; sprinkle with cheese and paprika.
6. Bake 10 minutes longer.

Pork-Stuffed Cabbage Rolls

Serves 6

1 medium cabbage
2 quarts plus ¼ cup boiling water
1½ teaspoons salt
½ teaspoon dill weed
⅛ teaspoon pepper
1½ pounds ground pork
1 small onion, chopped
¼ cup minced celery
1 egg
1 can (11 ounces) condensed Cheddar cheese soup
1 cup cooked rice
flour for gravy (optional)
paprika (optional)

1. Cut core from cabbage, place head in saucepan and add 2 cups boiling water; cook 3 to 4 minutes.
2. Drain cabbage; remove and reserve 12 leaves as they become flexible.
3. Sprinkle salt, dill weed and pepper over ground pork.
4. Add onion, celery, egg and ½ cup of cheese soup; stir lightly to combine.
5. Stir in cooked rice.
6. Divide meat mixture into 12 equal parts; place 1 portion of meat mixture on each cabbage leaf.
7. Roll leaves and fold ends to enclose filling; place rolls, seam-side down, in a large frying pan. (Rolls can be secured with small round wooden picks, if necessary.)
8. Add ¼ cup boiling water; cover tightly and cook 30 minutes.
9. Add remaining cheese soup; cook, covered, 10 minutes, or until cabbage and pork are done.
10. Remove rolls to warm platter; thicken cheese sauce with flour, if desired, and serve over rolls.
11. Sprinkle with paprika if desired.

Fruit-Stuffed Pork Roast

Serves 6 to 8

2 cups dried mixed fruit
1 cup dry sherry
4- to 5-pound boned and rolled pork loin or shoulder roast
1 package (1½ ounces) pot roast seasoning mix

1. Marinate dried fruit in sherry 1 to 2 hours.
2. Drain and reserve sherry.
3. Untie roast; stuff with fruit. Retie.
4. Rub roast thoroughly with seasoning mix.
5. Place roast on a rack in a shallow roasting pan. (Insert meat thermometer in center of roast if desired.)
6. Place roast in preheated 400° F. oven 30 minutes.
7. Reduce heat to 325° F. and continue roasting approximately 30 minutes per pound, or 170° F. on meat thermometer.
8. Baste with reserved sherry during the last 30 minutes of roasting time.
9. Let stand 10 minutes before slicing.

Pork Shoulder with Grapefruit Stuffing

Serves 6 to 8

- 2 tablespoons butter or margarine
- ¼ cup chopped celery
- ¼ cup chopped onion
- 12 slices raisin bread, crumbled
- 2 cups diced grapefruit sections
- 1 egg, beaten
- ¼ teaspoon dried rosemary
- ½ teaspoon salt
- ¼ teaspoon pepper
- 5 pounds boned pork shoulder

1. Melt butter in a small skillet; sauté celery and onion until tender.
2. Combine in a large bowl sautéed vegetables, bread crumbs, grapefruit, egg, rosemary, salt and pepper; mix well.
3. Spread stuffing over lean side of meat; roll up meat and tie securely.
4. Place meat on a roasting rack in a shallow pan, fat-side up.
5. Insert meat thermometer into meat (not stuffing).
6. Roast in preheated 325° F. oven 3 to 3½ hours, or until meat thermometer registers 185° F.
7. Let stand 15 minutes before slicing.

Finnish Pork Pot Pie

Serves 8

- 2 tablespoons butter or margarine
- 1 package (about 10 ounces) pie crust mix
- 1 cup sour cream
- 2 eggs, slightly beaten
- 2 pounds ground pork
- 1 can (10¾ ounces) condensed cream of mushroom soup
- 1 cup shredded Swiss cheese
- ¼ cup chopped onion
- ¼ cup chopped parsley
- ¼ teaspoon salt
- ⅛ teaspoon pepper
- 2 to 4 tablespoons milk

1. To make crust, cut butter into pie crust mix in a bowl until mixture resembles coarse cornmeal.
2. Add ½ cup sour cream and 1 egg.
3. Divide mixture in half; cover and chill overnight.
4. On a lightly floured board, roll each half into an 11-inch circle; line a 9-inch pie plate with one circle, trimming to fit the pie plate.
5. To make the filling, brown pork in a large skillet, stirring to separate meat; pour off fat.
6. Add ½ can soup, cheese, onion, parsley, salt and pepper.
7. Spoon into pie shell; top with remaining pastry, sealing and trimming edges.
8. Prick top with a fork; brush with remaining egg. (Garnish with additional pastry if desired.)
9. Bake in preheated 375° F. oven 45 minutes, or until brown.
10. Meanwhile, heat remaining soup, sour cream and milk in a saucepan; serve with pie.

MAINDISH FARE   PORK

Angostura Lasagna Rolls

Serves 6

- 1 pound Italian sweet sausage or 1 pound ground lean chuck
- 1 envelope soybean protein meat extender (optional)
- 1 tablespoon Angostura aromatic bitters
- 2 eggs
- ½ cup dry bread crumbs
- ½ cup (about) water
- 1 package (10 ounces) frozen chopped spinach, thawed and squeezed dry
- 12 lasagna noodles (8 ounces)
- boiling salted water
- 2 jars (15½ ounces each) marinara sauce
- ⅓ cup grated Parmesan cheese

1. Fry sausage in a skillet until brown and crumbly; drain excess fat.
2. Stir in meat extender, bitters, eggs, bread crumbs and enough water to make a thick mixture.
3. Stir in spinach.
4. Cook lasagna noodles in boiling salted water 15 minutes; drain and rinse with cold water.
5. Place noodles in single strips side by side on a towel.
6. Spread strips with meat filling; roll up each strip like a jelly roll.
7. Place rolls, upright, in a greased straight-sided, 3-inch-deep, 2-quart casserole.
8. Spoon sauce over lasagna rolls, allowing it to run down into noodles; sprinkle with cheese.
9. Bake, covered, in a preheated 350° F. oven 35 to 40 minutes.
10. Serve with additional grated Parmesan cheese.

Roly-Poly Pork Loaves with Corn Bread Stuffing

Makes 2 loaves, 6 to 8 servings each

- 3 pounds ground pork
- 1 can (8 ounces) tomato sauce
- 1 egg
- ¼ cup minced green pepper
- 2 teaspoons salt
- 2 teaspoons chili powder
- ⅛ teaspoon pepper
- Corn Bread Stuffing
- 2 tablespoons catsup

1. Combine pork, tomato sauce, egg, green pepper and seasonings.
2. Pat out half the mixture on waxed paper into a 10 × 8-inch rectangle.
3. Place half the stuffing in a layer over the meat, pressing lightly.
4. Roll up from the short end, jelly-roll fashion, to form a loaf; seal ends.
5. Place, seam-side down, on the rack in a roasting pan; bake in preheated 350° F. oven 1¼ hours.
6. Spread with catsup; bake 5 to 10 minutes.
7. Prepare second loaf; freeze, wrap and store at 0° F. or below for 2 to 3 weeks. (To cook frozen loaf, bake as directed, increasing original time to 1½ to 1¾ hours.)

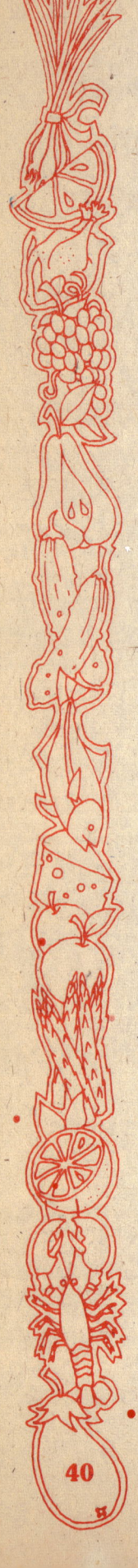

Corn Bread Stuffing

1 package (8½ ounces) corn muffin mix
¼ cup minced onion
½ cup minced celery
1 tablespoon butter or margarine
1 teaspoon sage
¼ cup water

1. Make corn bread according to package directions; cool and crumble.
2. Brown onion and celery in butter; stir in corn bread, sage and water.

Swiss Vegetable Roll with Mustard Sauce

Serves 6 to 8

1 cup plus 1 tablespoon mayonnaise-type salad dressing, divided
1 package (16 ounces) frozen broccoli Florentine (contains broccoli, carrots and onions)
1 cup shredded Swiss cheese
¼ cup chopped green onion
1 can (6½ ounces) chunk ham, drained
2 tablespoons all-purpose flour
1 cup milk
12 eggs, separated
½ teaspoon salt
⅛ teaspoon pepper
Mustard Sauce

1. Line a 15½ × 10½ × 1-inch jelly-roll pan with wax paper; brush with 1 tablespoon salad dressing.
2. Cook vegetables half the time recommended on package directions; cool.
3. Chop vegetables into fine pieces; combine with cheese, onion, ham and ½ cup salad dressing.
4. Combine remaining salad dressing with flour; gradually add milk and beaten egg yolks.
5. Cook, stirring constantly, over low heat until thickened; cool 15 minutes.
6. Fold egg yolk mixture, salt and pepper into stiffly beaten egg whites; pour into jelly-roll pan.
7. Bake in preheated 425° F. oven 20 minutes.
8. Invert pan on towel.
9. Spread vegetable mixture over omelet roll. (Save any leftover for sauce.)
10. Roll from narrow end, lifting with towel while rolling.
11. Serve, seam-side down; top with Mustard Sauce.

Mustard Sauce

1 cup salad dressing
2 tablespoons mustard
2 teaspoons sugar

Blend together well.

Tasty Pork Turnovers

Serves 6

1½ pounds ground pork
1½ teaspoons salt
¼ teaspoon ground savory
⅛ teaspoon pepper
1 cup chopped cooked potatoes

¾ cup chopped cooked carrots
1 large onion, chopped
¼ cup sweet pickle relish
¼ cup catsup
Pastry for Turnovers

1. Brown pork in a large frying pan; pour off drippings.
2. Sprinkle salt, savory and pepper over meat.
3. Add potatoes, carrots, onion, sweet pickle relish and catsup; stir lightly to combine.
4. Divide Pastry for Turnovers in half; roll each portion into an 11 × 16½-inch rectangle.
5. Cut each rectangle into six 5½-inch squares.
6. Place approximately ⅓ cup meat mixture in center of each pastry square; brush edges with water.
7. Fold each pastry square into a triangle; press edges together with a fork.
8. Place turnovers on baking sheets; bake in preheated 425° F. oven 30 minutes, or until pastry is lightly browned.
9. Remove from pan immediately; place on wire rack.

Pastry for Turnovers

3½ cups flour
2 teaspoons salt

1 cup lard
½ to ⅔ cup ice water

1. Mix flour and salt.
2. Cut lard into flour mixture with fork or pastry blender until crumbs are about the size of small peas.
3. Add ice water, a small amount at a time, mixing quickly and evenly until dough just holds in a ball.

Sausage Links in Batter Pudding

Serves 5 to 6

1 pound fresh pork
   sausage links
2 tablespoons water

2 cups milk
½ cup yellow cornmeal
1 teaspoon salt

4 eggs, well beaten

1. Place sausage links in a cold frying pan; add water, cover tightly and cook slowly 5 minutes. Set aside.
2. Heat milk in a double boiler or heavy saucepan; add cornmeal and salt, cooking slowly, stirring constantly, 10 to 15 minutes, or until thickened.
3. Cool slightly; add eggs, stirring to blend.
4. Pour mixture into a greased utility 13 × 9-inch dish; arrange sausage links on top.
5. Bake in preheated 325° F. oven 40 to 50 minutes, or until golden brown.
6. Serve immediately.

Roasted Potatoes & Sausage Under Wraps

Serves 6

- 6 large Idaho potatoes, peeled
- 1 pound bulk sausage meat
- 1 tablespoon Angostura aromatic bitters
- 3 tablespoons minced onion
- ⅓ cup dry bread crumbs
- salt to taste
- pepper to taste
- 6 slices lean bacon

1. With apple corer, hollow out potatoes lengthwise.
2. Mix together sausage, bitters, onion and crumbs in a bowl until well blended.
3. Use mixture to stuff holes in potatoes. (If any sausage mixture remains, shape into 1-inch balls and set aside.)
4. Sprinkle potatoes with salt and pepper.
5. Place, side by side, in a well-greased shallow baking pan; cover with foil.
6. Bake in preheated 350° F. oven 50 minutes, or until tender.
7. Remove cover; put bacon slices over tops of potatoes so they are covered.
8. Add sausage balls; bake 15 to 20 minutes longer, or until bacon is brown and crisp.
9. Serve potatoes with sausage balls.

Stuffed Pork Butterfly Chops

Serves 6

- 6 butterfly pork chops, cut 1 to 1¼-inches thick
- ¼ pound fresh pork sausage
- ¼ cup minced celery
- ¼ cup minced onion
- 2 cups semi-soft bread cubes
- ¼ teaspoon salt
- ¼ teaspoon sage
- 3 tablespoons water
- 2 tablespoons lard or drippings
- salt (optional)
- pepper (optional)

1. Make pockets in each chop by cutting into each side ("wing") of chop (parallel to surface of chop), beginning at center and cutting toward fat edge, but not to edge.
2. Lightly brown sausage in a frying pan, separating into small pieces.
3. Add celery and onion; cook 5 to 10 minutes.
4. Combine sausage mixture with bread cubes, salt and sage.
5. Add water, mixing thoroughly.
6. Fill both pockets in each chop with 1½ to 2 tablespoons stuffing mixture.
7. Brown chops in lard, browning unstuffed side first.
8. Place in a baking dish or 13 × 9-inch roasting pan; cover with foil, securing edges around rim of pan.
9. Bake in preheated 350° F. oven 45 minutes.
10. Uncover and continue baking 15 minutes, or until done.
11. Season with salt and pepper if desired.

Foiled Chicken Supreme

Serves 4

1 cup rice
1 medium onion, minced
½ cup minced green pepper
1 teaspoon salt
¼ teaspoon pepper
1½ cups water

2 chicken breasts, split in half
1 can (10¾ ounces) condensed cream of mushroom soup
½ cup milk
1 package (10 ounces) frozen green beans

1. Mix together rice, onion, green pepper, salt, pepper and water in a bowl.
2. Tear 4 pieces of foil, each 16 inches long; equally divide rice mixture into center of each piece of foil. (Turn edges up so liquid doesn't run out.)
3. Place chicken on top of rice mixture.
4. Blend together soup and milk; spoon over chicken.
5. Thaw beans only enough to separate them; arrange beans around chicken.
6. Bring long ends of foil together and double fold ends; fold other two ends up so juices do not run out.
7. Place foil packages on cookie sheet in preheated 375° F. oven; bake 1 hour.
8. Serve in foil.

Sherried Chicken-Filled Crêpes

Serves 6

4 tablespoons butter or margarine
2½ cups (½ pound) sliced mushrooms
⅓ cup minced onion
¼ cup flour
2 cups milk
1½ teaspoons original Worcestershire sauce

2 chicken bouillon cubes
¾ teaspoon salt
½ cup dairy sour cream
2 tablespoons dry sherry
2 cups chunked cooked chicken
3 tablespoons finely chopped parsley, divided
12 Crêpes

1. Melt butter in a large skillet.
2. Add mushrooms and onion; sauté 5 minutes.
3. Blend in flour; cook and stir 2 minutes.
4. Add milk, Worcestershire sauce, bouillon cubes and salt; cook, stirring over low heat until mixture thickens.
5. Stir in sour cream and sherry.
6. Remove 1 cup sauce; set aside and keep warm.
7. Add chicken and 2 tablespoons parsley to remaining sauce; heat until hot.
8. Heat Crêpes, tightly covered, in preheated 350° F. oven 10 minutes.
9. Spoon ¼ cup chicken mixture onto each crêpe; roll up.
10. Place two filled crêpes on each individual serving dish.

POULTRY MAINDISH FARE

11. Spoon 2 tablespoons reserved hot sauce over each portion; sprinkle with remaining parsley.
12. Serve immediately.

Crêpes

Makes 12

- 2 eggs
- ⅔ cup milk
- 1 tablespoon butter or margarine, melted
- ½ cup all-purpose flour
- ¼ teaspoon salt
- corn oil

1. Beat eggs thoroughly in a medium-size mixing bowl; stir in milk and butter.
2. Blend in flour and salt just until smooth.
3. Lightly brush a 5-inch crêpe pan with oil; heat over medium heat.
4. Add 2 measuring tablespoons of batter, tilting pan so batter covers bottom completely; cook 2 minutes on each side, or until golden.
5. Repeat with remaining batter.
6. Pile crêpes on top of each other on a plate. (Crêpes may be freezer-wrapped and stored in freezer until needed.)

Tortellini

Makes approximately 45 tortellini

- 1 cup minced, cooked chicken
- ¼ cup grated Parmesan cheese
- 1 egg, separated
- ⅛ teaspoon grated lemon peel
- ⅛ teaspoon ground nutmeg
- 1 teaspoon lemon pepper seasoning
- seasoned salt to taste
- 1 package (12 ounces) won ton skins, small size (3-inch square)
- 6 to 8 quarts boiling salted water
- 1 package (1½ ounces) spaghetti sauce mix with imported mushrooms, prepared according to package directions

1. Mix together chicken, Parmesan cheese, 1 egg yolk, lemon peel, nutmeg and lemon pepper seasoning; blend well.
2. Add seasoned salt to taste.
3. Cut a 2-inch-diameter circle in each won ton skin.
4. Place ¼ teaspoon filling in center of each circle; moisten edges with beaten egg white.
5. Fold each circle in half; press edges together.
6. Shape into little rings by stretching the tips of each half-circle slightly and wrapping the ring around index finger; gently press tips together.
7. Drop tortellini into boiling water; cook about 8 minutes, or until tender. (Do a few at a time, so they don't stick together.)
8. Drain; serve at once, topped with spaghetti sauce.

Chicken Breasts Stuffed with Herb Wheat Germ

Serves 4

½ cup vacuum-packed wheat germ, regular
¼ cup chopped green onion
½ teaspoon basil, crumbled
¼ teaspoon garlic powder
butter or margarine
2 teaspoons chicken stock
2 tablespoons flour
¾ cup dry white wine
½ cup half and half
2 whole chicken breasts, halved and boned

1. Combine wheat germ, onion, basil and garlic powder with ¼ cup melted butter; set aside.
2. Mix stock and flour; gradually add wine and half and half, stirring until smooth.
3. Blend 1 tablespoon sauce with wheat germ mixture; set remaining sauce aside.
4. Place chicken breasts skin-side down; cover with waxed paper and flatten with mallet.
5. Place an equal amount of wheat germ stuffing on each chicken piece; roll up and fasten with toothpicks.
6. Brown roll-ups in 1 tablespoon butter in skillet; transfer to a 1½-quart baking dish.
7. Pour remaining wine sauce over chicken; cover and bake in preheated 400° F. oven 40 to 45 minutes, or until tender.
8. Remove toothpicks before serving.

Folded Stuffed Chicken with Lemon Barbecue Sauce

Serves 6

3 cleaned broiler-fryer chickens, weighing 3 pounds each, halved
salt
1½ cups soft bread crumbs
½ cup chopped nuts
3 chicken livers, chopped
2 tablespoons chopped parsley
3 tablespoons butter or margarine, melted
2 teaspoons original Worcestershire sauce

Lemon Barbecue Sauce

1. Sprinkle chicken with salt.
2. Combine remaining ingredients except Lemon Barbecue Sauce.
3. Place a heaping spoonful of stuffing mixture on inside of chicken breast.
4. Break backbone and fold leg over stuffing; tie leg and wing together.
5. Brush with Lemon Barbecue Sauce.
6. Place on a rack over a slow charcoal fire; grill until chicken is done, about 40 to 50 minutes, turning and basting occasionally with Lemon Barbecue Sauce.
7. Or, if desired, arrange chicken on rack in a broiler pan; brush with Lemon Barbecue Sauce and place under a preheated 375° F. broiler, following preceding directions for cooking.

11. Spoon 2 tablespoons reserved hot sauce over each portion; sprinkle with remaining parsley.
12. Serve immediately.

Crêpes

Makes 12

- 2 eggs
- 2/3 cup milk
- 1 tablespoon butter or margarine, melted
- 1/2 cup all-purpose flour
- 1/4 teaspoon salt
- corn oil

1. Beat eggs thoroughly in a medium-size mixing bowl; stir in milk and butter.
2. Blend in flour and salt just until smooth.
3. Lightly brush a 5-inch crêpe pan with oil; heat over medium heat.
4. Add 2 measuring tablespoons of batter, tilting pan so batter covers bottom completely; cook 2 minutes on each side, or until golden.
5. Repeat with remaining batter.
6. Pile crêpes on top of each other on a plate. (Crêpes may be freezer-wrapped and stored in freezer until needed.)

Tortellini

Makes approximately 45 tortellini

- 1 cup minced, cooked chicken
- 1/4 cup grated Parmesan cheese
- 1 egg, separated
- 1/8 teaspoon grated lemon peel
- 1/8 teaspoon ground nutmeg
- 1 teaspoon lemon pepper seasoning
- seasoned salt to taste
- 1 package (12 ounces) won ton skins, small size (3-inch square)
- 6 to 8 quarts boiling salted water
- 1 package (1 1/2 ounces) spaghetti sauce mix with imported mushrooms, prepared according to package directions

1. Mix together chicken, Parmesan cheese, 1 egg yolk, lemon peel, nutmeg and lemon pepper seasoning; blend well.
2. Add seasoned salt to taste.
3. Cut a 2-inch-diameter circle in each won ton skin.
4. Place 1/4 teaspoon filling in center of each circle; moisten edges with beaten egg white.
5. Fold each circle in half; press edges together.
6. Shape into little rings by stretching the tips of each half-circle slightly and wrapping the ring around index finger; gently press tips together.
7. Drop tortellini into boiling water; cook about 8 minutes, or until tender. (Do a few at a time, so they don't stick together.)
8. Drain; serve at once, topped with spaghetti sauce.

Chicken Breasts Stuffed with Herb Wheat Germ

Serves 4

½ cup vacuum-packed wheat germ, regular
¼ cup chopped green onion
½ teaspoon basil, crumbled
¼ teaspoon garlic powder
butter or margarine
2 teaspoons chicken stock
2 tablespoons flour
¾ cup dry white wine
½ cup half and half
2 whole chicken breasts, halved and boned

1. Combine wheat germ, onion, basil and garlic powder with ¼ cup melted butter; set aside.
2. Mix stock and flour; gradually add wine and half and half, stirring until smooth.
3. Blend 1 tablespoon sauce with wheat germ mixture; set remaining sauce aside.
4. Place chicken breasts skin-side down; cover with waxed paper and flatten with mallet.
5. Place an equal amount of wheat germ stuffing on each chicken piece; roll up and fasten with toothpicks.
6. Brown roll-ups in 1 tablespoon butter in skillet; transfer to a 1½-quart baking dish.
7. Pour remaining wine sauce over chicken; cover and bake in preheated 400° F. oven 40 to 45 minutes, or until tender.
8. Remove toothpicks before serving.

Folded Stuffed Chicken with Lemon Barbecue Sauce

Serves 6

3 cleaned broiler-fryer chickens, weighing 3 pounds each, halved
salt
1½ cups soft bread crumbs
½ cup chopped nuts
3 chicken livers, chopped
2 tablespoons chopped parsley
3 tablespoons butter or margarine, melted
2 teaspoons original Worcestershire sauce

Lemon Barbecue Sauce

1. Sprinkle chicken with salt.
2. Combine remaining ingredients except Lemon Barbecue Sauce.
3. Place a heaping spoonful of stuffing mixture on inside of chicken breast.
4. Break backbone and fold leg over stuffing; tie leg and wing together.
5. Brush with Lemon Barbecue Sauce.
6. Place on a rack over a slow charcoal fire; grill until chicken is done, about 40 to 50 minutes, turning and basting occasionally with Lemon Barbecue Sauce.
7. Or, if desired, arrange chicken on rack in a broiler pan; brush with Lemon Barbecue Sauce and place under a preheated 375° F. broiler, following preceding directions for cooking.

Lemon Barbecue Sauce

Makes about 1 cup

- ¾ cup bottled Italian salad dressing
- ¼ cup fresh lemon juice
- 1 tablespoon original Worcestershire sauce
- ¼ cup minced onion

Combine all ingredients.

Cannelloni Supreme

Serves 4 to 6

- 2 tablespoons butter or margarine
- 1 cup milk
- 2 eggs, well beaten
- ½ cup sifted all-purpose flour
- 1 teaspoon baking powder
- salt
- ½ pound ground pork
- 1 package (16 ounces) frozen Broccoli Florentine (contains broccoli, carrots and onions)
- 1 cup finely chopped cooked chicken
- ¼ cup grated Romano or Parmesan cheese
- ⅛ teaspoon thyme
- pepper to taste
- Sauce

1. Melt butter in milk; cool slightly.
2. Add eggs, flour, baking powder, and ½ teaspoon salt; mix until smooth.
3. Drop by tablespoonfuls into hot buttered skillet. (Makes about sixteen 5-inch pancakes.)
4. Fry each pancake on both sides until browned; remove and set aside to cool.
5. Brown pork in a skillet; drain excess fat.
6. Prepare Broccoli Florentine according to package directions; drain and set aside.
7. Combine broccoli, pork, chicken, cheese, thyme and salt and pepper to taste.
8. Spoon 2 tablespoons mixture in center of each pancake; roll up and put in shallow baking dish, seam-side up.
9. Pour Sauce over filled cannelloni; broil about 5 minutes, or until browned and heated through.

Sauce

- 3 tablespoons butter or margarine
- 3 tablespoons all-purpose flour
- 1½ cups half and half
- ½ cup grated Parmesan cheese
- white pepper to taste

1. Melt butter in a small saucepan; blend in flour.
2. Gradually stir in half and half; continue stirring until mixture is thickened.
3. Stir in Parmesan cheese; adjust seasoning.

Avocado Chicken Breasts

Serves 4

- 2 large chicken breasts, skinned, boned and cut in half
- 1 large avocado, peeled and pitted
- 2 tablespoons freshly squeezed lemon juice
- 5 teaspoons minced onion
- ½ cup grated Muenster cheese
- 1 egg, beaten
- ½ cup packaged dry bread crumbs
- 1 teaspoon salt
- 3 tablespoons butter or margarine

1. Pound chicken with meat mallet to ¼-inch thickness.
2. Cut avocado in half; slice one of the halves into 8 slices.
3. Dip slices in lemon juice; remove and set aside.
4. Rub remaining avocado half with lemon juice; set aside.
5. Sprinkle remaining lemon juice over chicken.
6. Sprinkle 1 teaspoon onion on each chicken piece; top with 2 tablespoons cheese and 2 slices avocado.
7. Fold breasts in half lengthwise, pinching edges together; dip in egg then in bread crumbs mixed with salt.
8. Melt butter in a large skillet; brown chicken on both sides over low heat, about 20 minutes.
9. Mash remaining avocado half with remaining 1 teaspoon onion; season to taste. Serve with chicken breasts.

Chicken Flautas with Guacamole con Cilantro

Makes 12 flautas

- 3 cups (about ¾ pound) shredded or diced cooked chicken
- 1 package chicken taco seasoning mix
- 1 cup water
- 1 dozen (8-inch) flour tortillas
- salad oil for frying
- dairy sour cream

Guacamole con Cilantro

1. Combine chicken, taco seasoning mix and water in a large skillet; bring to a boil.
2. Reduce heat and simmer, uncovered, 10 minutes; set aside.
3. Heat ½-inch oil in a large skillet to about 375° F.
4. On each flour tortilla, place 1 to 2 tablespoons of prepared chicken filling in a long strip; roll up tightly to form a tube (like a crêpe).
5. Hold flap firmly with tongs and place in hot oil; hold until flap fries firmly closed.
6. Lightly brown all sides; remove and drain on paper towels.
7. Serve immediately topped with sour cream and guacamole.

Guacamole con Cilantro

Makes 3 cups

- 2 medium-size ripe avocados, peeled
- 1 tablespoon lemon juice
- 2 medium-size tomatoes, peeled and finely chopped
- 1 cup minced onion
- 1½ teaspoons seasoned salt
- ½ teaspoon seasoned pepper
- 1 tablespoon chopped cilantro

1. Mash avocados with a fork; add lemon juice and blend.
2. Add remaining ingredients; combine thoroughly.

NOTE: The word "flauta" describes the flute shape of these filled and rolled tortillas.

Vegetable-Chicken Pockets

Serves 4

- ½ pound fresh mushrooms
- ½ pound fresh spinach
- 4 tablespoons corn oil
- ½ cup chopped onion
- 1 garlic clove, crushed
- ½ teaspoon oregano leaves, crushed
- pinch of pepper
- 4 boned and skinned chicken breasts
- 3 tablespoons dry white wine
- chopped parsley
- lemon wedges (optional)

1. Rinse, pat-dry and chop mushrooms; set aside.
2. Wash spinach; place in saucepan and cook, covered, only with the water clinging to the leaves until barely wilted.
3. Drain spinach well, squeezing out excess water; chop and set aside.
4. Heat 2 tablespoons oil in a skillet until hot; add onion and mushrooms, and sauté until tender.
5. Add garlic, oregano, pepper and spinach; cook and stir 1 minute. Set aside.
6. Meanwhile, flatten each chicken breast by placing between 2 sheets of wax paper or plastic wrap; pound with mallet or rolling pin until ¼-inch thick.
7. Spoon one-fourth of mushroom mixture onto center of each chicken breast; roll lengthwise and secure with wooden picks.
8. Place rolled-up breasts in a 9-inch-square shallow baking pan.
9. Combine wine with remaining corn oil; spoon over chicken.
10. Bake, uncovered, in preheated 400° F. oven, basting frequently, until chicken is tender, 15 to 20 minutes.
11. Sprinkle with parsley; serve with lemon wedges if desired.

Mexican Chicken Kiev

Serves 4

- 4 whole chicken breasts, halved, boned and skin removed
- 1 can (7 ounces) whole green chilies, rinsed and seeds removed
- ¼ pound Monterey Jack cheese
- ¼ cup grated Parmesan cheese
- ½ to 1 teaspoon chili powder
- ½ teaspoon garlic salt
- ¼ teaspoon cumin
- ¼ teaspoon seasoned pepper
- ½ cup fine dry bread crumbs
- 6 tablespoons butter, melted

1. Flatten chicken breasts with a meat mallet to ¼-inch thickness.
2. Cut chilies and Monterey Jack cheese in 8 pieces.
3. Place a piece of chile and cheese on each chicken breast; roll, tucking in sides.
4. Combine remaining ingredients except butter and bread crumbs.
5. Dip each chicken bundle in melted butter, then crumbs.
6. Place bundles, seam-side down, in a 13 × 9 × 2-inch baking dish without sides touching; drizzle with remaining butter.
7. Refrigerate at least ½ hour.
8. Bake, uncovered, in preheated 400° F. oven 20 to 25 minutes.

Mexican Rolls

Serves 4

- 2 whole chicken breasts, split, skinned and boned
- 1 can (4 ounces) whole green chilies
- 4 teaspoons chopped olives
- ½ cup shredded Monterey Jack cheese
- 1 egg, lightly beaten
- 1 cup crushed tortilla chips
- ¼ cup corn oil
- 1 envelope (1⅝) enchilada sauce mix
- ½ cup water
- 1 can (16 ounces) whole tomatoes, cut up
- ½ cup shredded aged Cheddar cheese

1. Pound chicken breasts to flatten.
2. On each breast, put 1 chile, 1 teaspoon chopped olives and 2 tablespoons Monterey Jack cheese; roll up breasts tightly and secure with wood picks.
3. Dip each roll into egg, then into crushed chips to coat.
4. Heat oil in skillet; brown chicken rolls lightly.
5. Place rolls in a shallow casserole dish.
6. Prepare enchilada sauce according to package directions, only using ½ cup water and undrained tomatoes; pour sauce over chicken rolls.
7. Bake in preheated 350° F. oven 35 to 40 minutes.
8. Sprinkle Cheddar cheese over top; bake 5 minutes longer, or until cheese is bubbly.

Mom's Chicken Croquettes with Peas

Serves 4 to 6

- 3 tablespoons butter or margarine
- ¼ cup flour
- ½ cup chicken stock
- ½ cup evaporated milk
- ½ teaspoon salt
- ¼ teaspoon freshly ground black pepper
- 1 teaspoon lemon juice
- ½ teaspoon grated onion
- 1 can (3½ ounces) button mushrooms, well-drained
- 2 cups cooked, minced chicken
- 1 small can (1½ ounces) chopped pimiento, well-drained
- 2 teaspoons minced parsley
- dash of nutmeg (optional)
- 1 egg yolk, beaten
- fresh cracker crumbs
- 1 egg, beaten
- corn oil for deep-fat frying
- 1 package (10 ounces) frozen peas, cooked

1. Melt butter in a large skillet.
2. Gradually stir in flour; cook and stir until butter-flour mixture is light brown.
3. Gradually stir in chicken stock and milk, stirring constantly over low heat; cook until thick.
4. Blend in remaining ingredients except cracker crumbs, whole egg, corn oil and peas; cook until very thick, about 1 minute, stirring.
5. Spread mixture on a plate to cool.
6. Shape into croquettes; dip in crumbs, egg and crumbs.
7. Fry croquettes in deep oil heated very hot; drain on paper towels.
8. Serve with hot cooked peas.

Mom's Turkey Pie

Serves 6

- 3 cups diced cooked turkey
- 2½ cups turkey gravy
- 1 cup flour
- 1 teaspoon baking powder
- 1 teaspoon salt
- ⅓ cup shortening
- ¼ cup hot water
- 2 teaspoons lemon juice

1 egg yolk, lightly beaten

1. Combine turkey with gravy; spread evenly in a greased 10-inch pie plate.
2. Combine flour, baking powder and salt in a bowl.
3. Mix together shortening, hot water, lemon juice and half the egg yolk; stir into flour mixture.
4. Chill.
5. Roll out dough for top; arrange crust over turkey mixture.
6. Cut slits in top of crust; brush crust with remaining egg yolk.
7. Bake in preheated 400° F. oven 25 to 30 minutes, or until crust is browned and gravy begins to bubble through.

VEGETARIAN DISHES

Stuffed Artichokes

Serves 4

4 artichokes
boiling water
2 tablespoons minced onion with green onion flakes
2 tablespoons grated Parmesan cheese
1 tablespoon capers, drained and minced
1 tablespoon minced parsley
½ teaspoon seasoned salt
¼ teaspoon seasoned pepper
¼ teaspoon garlic powder with parsley
1 cup fine dry bread crumbs
¾ pound bay shrimp (optional)
½ cup dry white wine or chicken stock
1 package Italian salad dressing mix, prepared according to package directions

1. Cut off stems and sharp tips of leaves on each artichoke.
2. Set artichokes in boiling water to cover; bring to a boil.
3. Reduce heat, cover and simmer 20 minutes; drain thoroughly.
4. Spread leaves apart carefully, reach inside with a small spoon, and scrape out the furry, inedible part.
5. Combine remaining ingredients except wine and salad dressing.
6. Divide mixture among artichokes, spooning into center and between leaves.
7. Place artichokes in a roasting pan to fit tightly; sprinkle 2 tablespoons wine or stock into each artichoke center.
8. Pour salad dressing over artichokes.
9. Cover and bake in preheated 350° F. oven 1 hour, basting with pan juices several times.

Cheese-Filled Pasta Shells

Serves 8

1 carton (15 ounces) ricotta cheese
1 cup shredded Monterey Jack cheese
2 cups shredded mozzarella cheese
½ cup grated Parmesan cheese
2 eggs, beaten
1 package (10 ounces) frozen chopped spinach, thawed and well drained
½ teaspoon salt
¼ teaspoon pepper
½ pound jumbo pasta shells
2 jars (15½ ounces each) meatless marinara sauce

1. Combine ricotta cheese, Monterey Jack cheese, 1 cup mozzarella cheese, Parmesan cheese, eggs, spinach, salt and pepper; set aside.
2. Cook pasta shells according to package directions; drain.
3. Fill shells with cheese mixture.
4. Spoon enough sauce into bottom of 2 greased medium-size baking dishes to cover; arrange half the stuffed shells in a single layer in each dish.
5. Spoon remaining sauce over shells; sprinkle ½ cup mozzarella cheese over top of shells in each dish.
6. Bake in preheated 350° F. oven 30 minutes.

VEGETARIAN DISHES

Bo-Peep Pie

Serves 6

1 cup chopped onion
1 medium-size green bell pepper, diced
1 tablespoon salad oil
1 pound broccoli, separated and cut into stems and flowerets
4 medium-size carrots, peeled and diced
1 can (8 ounces) tomato sauce
1 bay leaf
½ teaspoon basil
½ teaspoon seasoned salt
1 bunch Swiss chard or spinach, washed, trimmed and cut into bite-size pieces
2 tablespoons chopped parsley
2 cups mashed potatoes
paprika (for garnish)

1. Sauté onion and green pepper in oil in a large skillet.
2. Add broccoli, carrots, tomato sauce, bay leaf, basil and salt, stirring thoroughly.
3. Bring to a boil; cover, reduce heat, and simmer until vegetables are just tender, about 15 minutes.
4. Stir in chard or spinach.
5. Transfer vegetables to a 13 × 9 × 2-inch baking dish.
6. Blend parsley into potatoes; spread over top of vegetables.
7. Bake in preheated 350° F. oven 15 minutes.
8. Sprinkle with paprika before serving.

Zesty Cheese Strata

Serves 4

8 slices whole wheat bread
¾ cup shredded Gruyere or Swiss cheese
¼ cup chopped scallions
3 eggs, beaten lightly
1¼ cups milk
¼ cup mayonnaise
½ teaspoon Tabasco pepper sauce
½ teaspoon dried basil leaves, crumbled
¼ teaspoon salt
2 tomatoes, thinly sliced

1. Arrange four bread slices in the bottom of buttered 9 × 9-inch shallow baking dish.
2. Sprinkle with ½ cup cheese and scallions; top with remaining bread.
3. Combine eggs, milk, mayonnaise, Tabasco sauce, basil and salt in a small bowl; mix well.
4. Pour egg custard mixture over bread; press down so bread is covered with custard.
5. Cover and refrigerate 30 minutes.
6. Uncover; top with tomato slices and sprinkle with remaining cheese.
7. Bake in preheated 350° F. oven 30 to 35 minutes, or until knife inserted in custard comes out clean.
8. Let stand 10 minutes before serving.

VEGETARIAN DISHES

Eggs McMorice

Serves 1

butter
1 large egg
2 tablespoons milk
2 tablespoons grated Cheddar or Parmesan cheese
1 whole wheat pita bread

1. Heat 1 teaspoon butter in a small non-stick 7-inch skillet over medium heat until melted and sizzling.
2. Meanwhile, whisk egg with milk in a small bowl using a wire whip or fork; pour egg into skillet.
3. Reduce heat; cook gently, lifting edges to let uncooked mixture run underneath. Cook until just set.
4. Sprinkle egg with cheese; set aside.
5. Holding pita bread with tongs, place over gas flame, turning often, to heat and "puff."
6. Slice pita open around circumference of bread.
7. If desired, spread pita lightly on both sides with butter.
8. Slide omelet, open-face, onto one slice of pita bread; cover with remaining slice, cut in half and serve.

NOTE: For electric burners, place cake rack over burner. Turn burner on high and heat pita bread on rack, turning until bread "puffs."

Parisian Soufflé Roll-Up

Serves 8

6 tablespoons butter or margarine
¾ cup flour
¾ teaspoon salt
3½ cups milk
1½ cups shredded Swiss cheese
6 eggs, separated
1 package (16 ounces) frozen Vegetables Parisian (contains French-cut green beans, carrots, cauliflower and onions)
¼ teaspoon dry mustard

1. Grease a 15 × 10 × 1-inch jelly-roll pan, line with foil; grease foil and set aside.
2. Melt butter in a medium-size saucepan; blend in flour and salt.
3. Add 3 cups milk, stirring constantly until sauce thickens.
4. Remove from heat; pour 1 cup sauce into a small saucepan and set aside.
5. Add ½ cup cheese to remaining sauce; stir until cheese melts. Set aside to cool slightly.
6. Beat egg whites in a large bowl until soft peaks form; set aside.
7. Beat egg yolks in a large bowl until light and thick, about 3 minutes.
8. Stir a small amount of hot cheese sauce into yolks; slowly add remaining sauce, stirring until mixture is well blended.
9. Fold 1 cup egg whites into egg yolk mixture. (This will lighten the sauce.)

VEGETARIAN DISHES

10. Fold sauce gently into remaining egg whites.
11. Spread soufflé mixture evenly in greased, foil-lined pan; bake in preheated 325° F. oven 45 minutes, or until top is golden and springs back when touched.
12. While soufflé bakes, cook vegetables according to package directions; drain well.
13. Add dry mustard, ½ cup cheese, and remaining ½ cup milk to reserved sauce; stir over low heat until cheese melts.
14. When soufflé is done, remove from oven; loosen around edges.
15. Cover a cookie sheet with foil, place over soufflé, and turn soufflé upside down; remove jelly-roll pan and layer of foil carefully.
16. Spread vegetable mixture evenly over soufflé; sprinkle with remaining ½ cup cheese.
17. Pour ½ cup sauce over vegetables and cheese; starting at 10-inch side, roll, jelly-roll fashion, lifting foil to help guide soufflé.
18. Place on heated platter; spoon some of remaining sauce over top.
19. Cut roll into thick slices; serve with sauce.

Sam's Potato-Stuffed Omelet

Serves 4

For the Filling

1 cup chopped onion
¾ cup chopped green pepper
½ cup butter
3 potatoes, cooked and chopped
½ teaspoon salt
pinch of pepper

1. Sauté onion and green pepper in butter until tender.
2. Stir in potatoes; sprinkle with salt and pepper.
3. Spread mixture evenly in pan; cook slowly until bottom is browned.
4. Turn and brown the other side; set aside.

For the Omelet

8 eggs
¼ cup milk
½ teaspoon salt
¼ teaspoon pepper
4 tablespoons butter or margarine

1. Beat 2 eggs with 1 tablespoon milk, ⅛ teaspoon salt and a pinch of pepper.
2. Melt 1 tablespoon butter in medium-size skillet; heat until bubbly.
3. Pour egg mixture into skillet; let set around edges.
4. With pancake turner, gently lift edges as eggs set, tilting skillet to allow uncooked portion to run underneath and shaking skillet occasionally to keep omelet moving freely.
5. Spoon one-fourth potato filling over half the omelet; fold and turn out onto heated plate.
6. Repeat with remaining ingredients.

VEGETARIAN DISHES

Chile Rellenos

Serves 4 to 6

butter
1 can (4 ounces) whole green chilies, rinsed and seeded
1 cup chunky taco sauce
¼ pound sliced Cheddar cheese
¼ pound sliced Monterey Jack cheese
2 eggs, well beaten
4 teaspoons flour
1 can (5.3 ounces) evaporated milk

1. Arrange chilies in bottom of a lightly buttered 8 × 8 × 2-inch glass baking dish; top with ½ cup chunky taco sauce.
2. Layer the cheeses evenly on top of sauce.
3. Combine eggs, flour and milk in a small bowl, blending thoroughly; pour over cheese and chilies.
4. Bake in preheated 325° F. oven 25 to 30 minutes.
5. Remove from oven and spread remaining chunky taco sauce over top; bake 10 minutes longer.
6. Let stand about 5 minutes before cutting.

Tangy Broiled Tomato Halves

Serves 4

2 large tomatoes
2 tablespoons cracker crumbs
2 tablespoons prepared horseradish
1 tablespoon lemon juice
¼ teaspoon salt
¼ teaspoon paprika
2 teaspoons snipped parsley
3 tablespoons grated Parmesan cheese

1. Cut tomatoes in half crosswise.
2. Combine cracker crumbs, horseradish, lemon juice, salt and paprika.
3. Spread cracker mixture evenly over tomato halves; sprinkle with parsley and cheese.
4. Place on rack in broiler pan 2 to 3 inches from heat; broil 3 to 5 minutes, or just until heated.

Orange Shell Squash

Serves 4

1 package (12 ounces) frozen cooked squash
2 tablespoons brown sugar
2 tablespoons butter or margarine
½ teaspoon salt
pepper to taste
2 oranges, halved, pulp removed
4 large marshmallows

1. Cook squash according to package directions.
2. Add brown sugar, butter, salt and pepper; mix well.
3. Place one-fourth mixture in each orange shell.
4. Bake in preheated 350° F. oven 15 minutes.
5. Place marshmallows on top; heat until melted.

VEGETARIAN DISHES

Stuffed Tomatoes

Serves 6

6 large tomatoes
½ pound ground beef (optional)
½ cup chopped onion
½ cup chopped green pepper
¼ cup dark corn syrup
1 tablespoon original Worcestershire sauce
1 teaspoon dried basil leaves
1 teaspoon salt
¼ teaspoon pepper
1 cup herb-seasoned stuffing mix
¼ cup grated Parmesan cheese
3 ounces mozzarella cheese, shredded (¾ cup)

1. Cut tops off tomatoes; scoop out pulp.
2. Chop tops and pulp; drain.
3. Brown beef, onion and pepper in a large skillet over medium heat about 5 minutes.
4. Add tomatoes, corn syrup, Worcestershire sauce, basil, salt and pepper; cook, stirring, for 10 minutes, or until thick and bubbly.
5. Remove from heat; add stuffing mix and Parmesan cheese.
6. Spoon into tomato shells.
7. Place tomatoes in 11 × 7 × 2-inch baking dish; top each tomato with 2 tablespoons mozzarella cheese.
8. Bake in preheated 350° F. oven 25 to 30 minutes, or until heated.

Stuffed Peppers, Angostura

Serves 6

6 large green peppers
boiling water
¾ pound ground beef (optional)
¾ pound ground pork (optional)
1 onion, chopped
4 large cooked potatoes, diced
2 teaspoons Angostura aromatic bitters
2 cups (8 ounces) grated sharp Cheddar cheese
1½ cups milk
salt to taste
pepper to taste

1. Slice tops from peppers; remove seeds.
2. Drop peppers into boiling water; cook 5 minutes.
3. Drain and cool.
4. Mix together beef, pork, onion, potatoes, Angostura bitters, cheese and milk.
5. Season to taste with salt and pepper.
6. Use meat mixture to stuff peppers.
7. Place peppers side by side in a shallow baking pan; add water until 1 inch deep.
8. Bake in preheated 350° F. oven 1 hour.

NOTE: If desired, serve with tomato sauce.

VEGETARIAN DISHES

Wheat Germ Ravioli with Spinach Filling

Makes 4 dozen ravioli

1 to 1¼ cups flour
⅓ cup regular wheat germ
½ teaspoon salt
2 eggs, slightly beaten
1 tablespoon milk

Spinach Filling
4 quarts boiling salted water
1 jar (15 ounces) spaghetti
   or marinara sauce
grated Parmesan cheese

1. Combine 1 cup flour, wheat germ and salt.
2. Mix in eggs and milk until dough forms a ball. (Work in extra flour if sticky.)
3. Turn out onto board; knead 3 to 5 minutes until smooth and elastic. (Flour hands and board only if necessary.)
4. Enclose dough in plastic wrap; chill ½ hour. (Dough may be refrigerated overnight.)
5. Divide pasta dough in half; cover one half with plastic wrap.
6. Roll out other half of dough on lightly floured surface to a 15-inch square; loosen dough and stretch gently as you roll.
7. Cut dough into three 5-inch strips; cover 2 strips with plastic wrap.
8. Lengthen 1 strip to 18 inches with a rolling pin.
9. Place 8 rounded teaspoonfuls of Spinach Filling along the center of the strip, leaving even spaces between mounds of filling; fold dough over to enclose.
10. Press dough tightly around filling, working from folded edge to force out air; trim long edge of dough with pastry wheel or fluted vegetable cutter.
11. Cut between mounds to separate ravioli; cover with plastic wrap.
12. Repeat with remaining dough and filling.
13. Drop ravioli into boiling salted water; return to a boil, stirring to separate ravioli. Boil gently 5 minutes.
14. Drain in colander; serve with spaghetti sauce and cheese.

Spinach Filling

½ cup chopped green onion
1 clove garlic, minced
½ teaspoon thyme leaves,
   crushed
2 tablespoons butter

¾ cup regular wheat germ
½ of 10-ounce package frozen
   chopped spinach
½ cup grated Parmesan cheese
¼ cup milk

1. Sauté onion, garlic and thyme in butter.
2. Remove from heat; stir in wheat germ, spinach, cheese and milk.

NOTE: To freeze ravioli: Seal uncooked filled ravioli in moisture-proof wrapping; freeze until ready to use. Drop ravioli into boiling salted water; return to a boil and boil gently 5 to 7 minutes.

VEGETARIAN DISHES

Spinach-Zucchini Boats

Serves 6

3 medium-size zucchini (about 1½ pounds)
salt
boiling water
2 tablespoons butter or margarine
3 tablespoons all-purpose flour
1 cup milk
1 package (10 ounces) frozen chopped spinach, cooked and well drained
1 can (4½ ounces) sliced mushrooms, drained
¼ teaspoon nutmeg
½ cup grated Parmesan cheese

1. Trim ends from zucchini; cook in salted boiling water 10 to 12 minutes.
2. Drain zucchini thoroughly.
3. Split zucchini in half lengthwise, scoop out flesh to within ½-inch of side to form boats, setting shells aside.
4. Chop flesh; set aside.
5. Melt butter in a saucepan; add flour, stirring briskly.
6. Add milk; cook until thickened, stirring constantly.
7. Add reserved chopped zucchini, spinach, mushrooms and nutmeg; stir until well combined. Remove from heat.
8. Place zucchini boats in a shallow baking dish; fill with spinach mixture and sprinkle with cheese.
9. Bake in preheated 350° F. oven 15 to 20 minutes, or until cheese melts and zucchini is tender.

Foiled Vegetable Toss, Grilled

Serves 4 to 6

6 cups cubed, peeled eggplant (about 1 pound)
1 medium-size green pepper, seeded and coarsely chopped
1 onion, peeled and chopped
few grains white pepper
1 tablespoon margarine
¼ teaspoon dried basil leaves, crumbled
2 ripe tomatoes, chopped
½ teaspoon salt

1. Cut 3 pieces of heavy-duty aluminum foil about 18 × 12 inches each.
2. Mix together eggplant, green pepper and onion in a bowl.
3. Divide mixture, spooning among pieces of foil.
4. Place 1 teaspoon margarine over vegetables on each piece of foil; sprinkle with basil.
5. Wrap securely.
6. Place packets on grill 3 to 4 inches from heat; cook 35 minutes.
7. Meanwhile, place tomatoes on a piece of foil; wrap securely.
8. Place tomatoes on grill during last 15 minutes of cooking time.
9. Remove vegetables from heat; toss together in a large bowl.
10. Season to taste with salt and pepper.

VEGETARIAN DISHES

Curry-Stuffed Onions

Serves 4

- 4 medium onions (about 1½ pounds)
- 3 tablespoons butter
- ½ cup chopped celery
- 1 cup shredded carrot
- 1½ tablespoons Dijon-style mustard
- ¾ teaspoon curry powder
- ¼ teaspoon Tabasco pepper sauce
- ⅓ cup chopped, tart apple
- ¼ cup raisins
- hot water

1. Peel onions; cut off one quarter of each onion from the top and trim root end, leaving it intact.
2. Using a large melon-ball scoop, remove centers of onions, leaving ¼-inch-thick shells.
3. Stand onion shells in saucepan with 1 inch boiling water; cover and steam 15 minutes.
4. Remove onion shells from saucepan; invert on wire rack, cool, and drain.
5. Finely chop onion centers. (You should have ½ cup chopped.)
6. Melt 3 tablespoons butter in a skillet; sauté chopped onion 3 minutes.
7. Add celery; cook 1 minute.
8. Stir in carrot, mustard, curry powder and Tabasco sauce; remove from heat.
9. Stir in apple and raisins.
10. Spoon stuffing into onion shells.
11. Arrange in small baking dish; pour hot water into baking dish to a depth of 1 inch.
12. Bake in preheated 325° F. oven 15 minutes, or until onions are heated through.

Baked Stuffed Zucchini

Serves 4

- 4 zucchini (about 2 pounds)
- 2 tablespoons butter
- 2 scallions, chopped
- ½ pound fresh mushrooms, chopped
- ½ cup chopped walnuts
- ½ cup grated cheese
- 1 cup fresh bread crumbs
- 4 eggs
- 2 tablespoons minced parsley
- 1 tablespoon chopped fresh basil
- salt to taste
- pepper to taste

1. Scrub zucchini; cut in half lengthwise.
2. Scoop out and reserve pulp, leaving shells ¼-inch thick.
3. Parboil shells 5 minutes.
4. Chop pulp; sauté in butter.
5. Add scallions and mushrooms; cook 3 minutes.
6. Add nuts; remove from heat.
7. Add crumbs and eggs beaten with herbs and seasonings; pile into zucchini shells and top with grated cheese.
8. Bake in buttered baking dish in ½-inch water, uncovered, in preheated 350° F. oven 30 minutes.

VEGETARIAN DISHES

Bean-Stuffed Tomatoes

Serves 6

1 can (16 ounces) cut green beans, drained, reserving ¼ cup liquid
1 tablespoon minced onion
1 tablespoon bacon bits
1 can (4½ ounces) sliced mushrooms
¼ cup low-calorie Italian dressing
¼ cup sliced green onion
¼ teaspoon salt
pepper to taste
6 medium-size tomatoes

1. Heat reserved bean liquid with onion and bacon bits; bring to a boil.
2. Add green beans; simmer 6 minutes. (Drain if needed.)
3. Combine green bean mixture, mushrooms, dressing, green onion, salt and pepper to taste; refrigerate 2 hours, tossing occasionally.
4. Cut tops off tomatoes; scoop out the pulp and save for another recipe. Leave a ¼-inch shell in each tomato.
5. Invert shells on paper towels; chill.
6. To serve, season shells with salt to taste; fill with bean mixture.

NOTE: An attractive accompaniment to meat.

Elsie's Eggplant Supreme

Serves 8

2 eggplant, cut in ½-inch-thick slices
salt
10 large cloves fresh garlic
½ cup flour
½ cup commercially prepared biscuit mix
1 teaspoon oregano, crushed
½ teaspoon coarse ground black pepper
1 egg
2 tablespoons water (approximately)
olive oil
salad oil (vegetable oil)

1. Place eggplant slices on paper towels in a single layer; sprinkle both sides with salt. Set aside for ½ hour.
2. Press 6 cloves garlic through garlic press into a medium-size mixing bowl; add flour, biscuit mix, oregano, pepper, egg and enough water to reach the consistency of pancake batter.
3. Pour oil into a large skillet to a depth of ¼ inch, using half olive oil and half salad oil; heat oil over medium heat.
4. Crush 4 cloves of garlic with flat edge of knife; add to oil, sautéeing until lightly browned.
5. Before removing cloves, press them against the skillet, using a fork to release oils from garlic into cooking oil.
6. Coat each eggplant slice with batter; fry, being careful not to brown too fast. (Do not burn.)
7. Serve immediately.

SALADS

Tuna Nicosia

Serves 4

4 oranges
1 can (6½ or 7 ounces) tuna, drained
½ cup diced cucumber
¼ cup sliced scallions
⅓ cup slivered almonds, toasted
½ cup dairy sour cream
¼ cup real mayonnaise
1 tablespoon white wine vinegar
1 teaspoon dried leaf tarragon, crumbled
¼ teaspoon salt
dash of pepper
cucumber slices

1. Slice tops from each orange, using tip of teaspoon as a guide to cut scalloped edges.
2. Remove half the pulp from each orange; set aside.
3. Combine tuna, cucumber, scallions, almonds and reserved orange pulp in a medium-size bowl; set aside.
4. Combine sour cream, mayonnaise, vinegar, tarragon, salt and pepper in a small bowl; mix well.
5. Add ½ cup sour cream mixture to tuna mixture; toss lightly.
6. Spoon salad into prepared orange shells; top with orange lids.
7. Serve with cucumber slices and remaining sour cream dressing.

Winter Grape & Seafood Salad with Chili Dressing

Serves 4

½ cup plus 1 tablespoon salad oil
4 flour tortillas
1½ cups red or green grapes
½ cup minced celery
¼ cup minced green or sweet red onion
2 tablespoons minced parsley
1 tablespoon lime juice
salt to taste
1½ cups cooked shrimp or 2 cans (4¼ ounces each) deveined shrimp, rinsed, or 1 can (4¼ ounces) shrimp and 1 can (7 ounces) solid-pack tuna, drained
1½ quarts shredded crisp lettuce
Chili Dressing

1. Heat ½ cup salad oil in a skillet to 375° F.; fry 4 flour tortillas, 1 at a time, until bubbly and golden on each side but still pliable.
2. Lift out tortillas and place in a wire strainer or over back of small bowl; let cool a minute to shape into a shallow bowl.
3. Rinse grapes; halve and seed if necessary.
4. Mix grapes with celery, onion, parsley, lime juice and 1 tablespoon oil; add salt to taste.

5. Gently mix in shrimp.
6. Divide lettuce on 4 large salad plates; top each with a tortilla shell and fill with shrimp mixture.
7. Serve with Chili Dressing.

Chili Dressing
Makes 1¼ cups

½ teaspoon chili powder
1 tablespoon wine vinegar
2 tablespoons orange juice
1 tablespoon mashed green chilies
1¼ cups mayonnaise

1. Blend chili powder with wine vinegar and orange juice.
2. Add green chilies; stir into mayonnaise.

Mexicali Corn Salad with Salsa Olé
Serves 4 to 6

4 ears of fresh corn
boiling salted water
1½ cups finely shredded red cabbage
1 large green pepper, chopped
1 large tomato, cubed
½ cup cooked, crumbled bacon
4 to 6 pita breads or taco shells
Salsa Olé
1½ cups shredded Cheddar cheese

1. Remove husks and silk from corn; snap off ends of stalks just before cooking.
2. Cook, covered, in boiling salted water to cover 5 to 7 minutes.
3. Drain and cool; cut corn off cob.
4. Combine cabbage, green pepper, tomato and bacon in a large bowl; stir in ¾ cup Salsa Olé, mixing well.
5. Cover and chill.
6. Fill pita bread or taco shells with corn mixture; top with remaining ½ cup Salsa Olé and shredded cheese.

Salsa Olé
Makes 1¼ cups sauce

1 cup dairy sour cream
3 tablespoons freshly squeezed lime juice
2 tablespoons minced onion
1 clove garlic, minced
1 teaspoon chili powder
1 teaspoon ground cumin
½ teaspoon sugar
¼ teaspoon salt
⅛ to ¼ teaspoon cayenne

Combine all ingredients in a small bowl; mix well.

FINGER FOOD

Calzone (Filled Bread)

Makes 6 to 8 main dish servings
or 12 appetizer servings

1 pound uncooked pizza dough
¼ cup soft butter
½ teaspoon garlic salt
⅛ teaspoon pinch of herbs
2 to 4 ounces sliced provolone cheese
2 to 4 ounces sliced mozzarella cheese
2 to 4 ounces sliced prosciutto
2 to 4 ounces sliced Italian ham
2 to 4 ounces salami
2 to 4 ounces salami cotto

1. Roll or pat out pizza dough on floured board to form rectangle approximately 14 × 8 inches; spread with half the soft butter mixture; add garlic salt and herbs.
2. Layer meats and cheeses on half the dough, lengthwise; fold pizza dough over filling, sealing at seams and ends.
3. Brush with remaining soft butter mixture.
4. Place on greased jelly-roll pan; bake in preheated 450° F. oven 20 minutes or until golden.

Falafel Patties

Serves 4

1 cup cooked chick peas
1 egg
¼ teaspoon dry mustard
¼ teaspoon garlic powder
dash of seasoned salt
2 tablespoons minced onion
¼ cup sesame or sunflower seeds, ground
2 tablespoons wheat germ
1 tablespoon bran
2 tablespoons soy nuts, ground
½ cup whole wheat bread crumbs (1 slice)
1 tablespoon corn oil
4 small pita bread pockets
shredded lettuce
mayonnaise or Yogurt Sauce

1. Purée chick peas in blender with egg; remove mixture to a bowl.
2. Stir in seasonings, minced onion, ground seeds, wheat germ, bran and ground soy nuts to distribute evenly.
3. Place bread crumbs in a shallow bowl or plate.
4. Divide batter into 8 patties 2¼ to 2½ inches in diameter; roll each patty in crumbs.
5. Heat oil in a non-stick skillet; brown patties, about 3 minutes on each side, over medium heat.
6. Serve 2 patties in each of four pita bread pockets with shredded lettuce and mayonnaise or Yogurt Sauce.

Yogurt Sauce

¼ cup plain yogurt
1 teaspoon prepared mustard
¼ cup mayonnaise

Blend all ingredients thoroughly in small bowl.

FINGER FOOD

Quarterback's Crescent Franks

Serves 8

8 slices bacon
1 package (8 ounces) refrigerated crescent rolls

8 wieners
1 can (8 ounces) pork and beans

1. Fry bacon until crisp; drain and crumble.
2. Divide dough into 8 triangles.
3. Spread 1 tablespoon pork and beans over each triangle; sprinkle with bacon.
4. Place 1 wiener at base of each triangle; roll up.
5. Put wiener rolls on ungreased cookie sheet; bake in preheated 375° F. oven 12 to 15 minutes, or until golden brown.

Peel Deals

frankfurter buns
melted butter or margarine
mustard
catsup

cheese
frankfurters
baked beans (optional)
pickle relish (optional)

chopped olives (optional)

1. Split frankfurter buns; brush inside and out with melted butter or margarine.
2. Spread cut sides with mustard or catsup; cover with a strip of cheese.
3. Place frankfurter in center of bun; top with drained baked beans, pickle relish, or chopped olives.
4. Wrap each filled bun in foil; place in preheated 375° F. oven 12 to 15 minutes, or until heated.

Deviled Corned Beef Buns

Serves 4

4 hot dog buns
½ cup shredded canned corned beef
½ cup grated process American cheese
⅓ cup chopped stuffed olives

¼ cup catsup
2 tablespoons minced green onions
1 tablespoon original Worcestershire sauce
1 teaspoon minced green pepper

1. Split buns and remove soft centers.
2. Combine remaining ingredients; fill rolls.
3. Wrap each roll in foil; twist ends.
4. Place buns in a large paper bag; twist end to close.
5. Heat in preheated 325° F. oven 20 minutes.

FINGER FOOD

Ham en Panier

Serves 6

6 large hard rolls
1½ cups ground cooked ham
3 hard-cooked eggs, chopped
1 teaspoon chopped parsley
1½ tablespoons butter or margarine

1 tablespoon flour
¼ teaspoon salt
⅛ teaspoon pepper
1½ cups milk
3 tablespoons prepared Dijon mustard

pimiento (optional garnish)

1. Cut a slice from the top of each roll; scoop out center of rolls.
2. Combine cooked ham, hard-cooked eggs and parsley; set aside.
3. Melt butter or margarine; stir in flour, salt and pepper.
4. Add milk, stirring constantly until thickened.
5. Add mustard.
6. Add ham and egg mixture to mustard sauce.
7. Fill buns with creamed mixture.
8. Heat rolls in a moderate 350° F. oven for 10 minutes.
9. Garnish with chopped pimiento if desired.

Ramada

Makes 4 sandwiches

16 slices very thinly sliced ham
4 whole green chilies (fresh or canned), seeds removed

4 slices cucumber
4 slices Monterey Jack cheese
4 tortillas

Arrange 4 ham slices and 1 slice of each of the remaining ingredients in center of each tortilla.

Mexican Monte Carlo Sandwich

Serves 6

2 cans (7 ounces each) green chile salsa
1¼ pounds ground beef
12 slices sour dough or French bread, ½-inch thick
1 can (7 ounces) whole green chilies, split

1 package (4 ounces) shredded Monterey Jack cheese
2 eggs, beaten
1 cup milk
butter or margarine

1. Combine 1 can salsa with beef; shape into 6 patties.
2. Broil until desired doneness.
3. Place patty on bread slice; top with chile, about 1 tablespoon cheese and bread slice.
4. Combine eggs and milk.

66

5. Dip both sides of sandwich in egg-milk mixture; cook sandwich in butter until golden on both sides. Heat remaining salsa; serve with sandwich.

Monte Cristo Sandwich

Serves 6

6 turkey slices
6 Swiss cheese slices
6 ham slices
12 white bread slices
Batter
corn oil for deep-fat frying
confectioner's sugar

1. Using 1 slice each of turkey, cheese and ham for each sandwich, make sandwich with white bread slices, placing cheese between turkey and ham.
2. Cut sandwich in quarters, using wooden picks to hold sandwich.
3. Dip quarters in batter; fry in oil, heated to 360° F. until golden.
4. Remove picks; sprinkle with confectioner's sugar.

Batter

Makes 3 cups

1½ cups flour
1 tablespoon baking powder
¼ teaspoon salt
1⅓ cups water
1 egg

1. Sift flour, baking powder and salt.
2. Add water to beaten egg.
3. Add egg to flour mixture; mix well.

Pâté en Croute

Makes two 12-inch loaves

2 loaves (12 inches each) Italian bread
1 pound chicken livers
1 cup chopped onions
1 small clove garlic, minced
¼ teaspoon ground thyme
¼ teaspoon ground allspice
½ cup margarine
2 tablespoons chopped parsley
1 tablespoon dry sherry (optional)

1. Cut each Italian bread loaf in half crosswise; hollow out centers, leaving ½-inch shell. Reserve soft bread crumbs.
2. Sauté livers, onions, garlic, thyme and allspice in margarine until livers are done.
3. Mix in parsley, sherry and reserved bread crumbs; in food processor or electric blender, blend mixture until smooth.
4. Fill hollowed bread with liver mixture; wrap in plastic wrap and chill 2 hours.
5. Slice in ½-inch-thick slices to serve.

NOTE: For Liver Pâté Spread, omit Italian bread loaves and add 2½ cups soft bread crumbs to liver mixture. Prepare as above. Makes 3½ cups.

FINGER FOOD

Mystery Loaf

Serves 6

½ pound lean ground beef
½ teaspoon seasoned salt
1 teaspoon chili powder
2 ripe California avocados
1 large oval-shaped French bread
garlic salt
1 can (8 ounces) refried beans, heated
shredded lettuce
bottled taco sauce (optional)
1 ripe tomato, sliced
2 sliced green onions
½ cup shredded sharp American cheese
corn chips (optional)

1. Brown beef, stirring until crumbly; drain fat.
2. Stir in salt and chili powder; keep hot.
3. Halve, slice and peel avocados; cut one into crescents and one into lengthwise slices.
4. Split French bread in half lengthwise; lightly toast cut side under broiler.
5. Arrange a layer of avocado crescents on bottom half of bread; sprinkle with garlic salt.
6. Spread an even layer of hot beans over avocado, followed by hot meat mixture.
7. Cover meat with shredded lettuce; if desired, sprinkle with taco sauce.
8. Cover with a layer of tomato slices; sprinkle with onions and cheese.
9. Arrange row of lengthwise avocado slices over all; sprinkle with garlic salt.
10. Cover with top half of bread; serve, cut into slices, with corn chips if desired.

Beef Loaf in a Loaf

Serves 8

1 loaf Vienna bread
2 pounds lean ground beef
1 egg
¼ cup chili sauce
3 tablespoons instant minced onion
3 tablespoons chopped green pepper
2 teaspoons salt
⅛ teaspoon pepper
4 slices (3 ounces) American cheese

1. Cut a shallow slice, 2½ inches wide, from the top of loaf of bread; remove bread to hollow out the inside of the loaf until sides and bottom are ½-inch thick.
2. Make 1 cup crumbs from removed bread; combine crumbs with beef, egg, chili sauce, minced onion, green pepper, salt and pepper.
3. Line bottom of inside of loaf with slices of cheese; add meat mixture, a portion at a time, pressing lightly to fill loaf.
4. Place top on loaf; wrap in foil, sealing top and ends.
5. Place loaf on rack in a large roasting pan; bake in preheated 350° F. oven 2 hours.
6. Let stand 10 minutes before slicing.

FINGER FOOD

Sausage Pockets

Serves 6

- 1 pound summer sausage, cut in bite-size pieces
- 1 small onion, sliced in rings
- 1 green bell pepper, cut in 1-inch pieces
- 1 can (2¼ ounces) sliced ripe olives
- 8 large mushrooms, sliced
- 1 package (1½ ounces) spaghetti sauce mix with imported mushrooms, prepared according to package directions
- 6 small rounds pita bread, sliced in half

1. Brown sausage, onion and green pepper in a large skillet until vegetables are almost tender; drain fat.
2. Add olives, mushrooms and spaghetti sauce; bring to a boil.
3. Reduce heat and simmer, uncovered, 10 minutes.
4. Fill each pita bread half with sausage-sauce mixture.

Nan's Nutty Pita Pockets

Serves 4

- 1 can (6½ or 7 ounces) chunk tuna, drained
- 1 cup shredded Cheddar cheese
- ½ cup chopped lettuce
- ⅓ cup coarsely chopped pecans
- ¼ cup diced celery
- ¼ cup chopped green onion
- real mayonnaise
- 1 teaspoon dill weed
- ½ teaspoon garlic salt
- 2 small pita bread rounds, cut in half

1. Combine cheese, lettuce, pecans, celery, green onion, ¼ cup mayonnaise, dill weed and garlic salt; fold in tuna.
2. Spread additional mayonnaise inside each pita round half if desired; spoon tuna mixture into pita round halves to serve.

Fried Reuben Sandwiches

Makes 8 sandwiches

- 8 slices Swiss cheese
- 1 pound thinly sliced corned beef
- 1 can (16 ounces) Bavarian-style sauerkraut, drained
- ½ cup Thousand Island dressing
- 16 slices rye bread
- 2 eggs, lightly beaten
- ⅓ cup milk
- ½ teaspoon sugar
- dash of salt
- 3 tablespoons butter or margarine, melted

1. Place Swiss cheese, corned beef, sauerkraut and 1 tablespoon dressing on 8 slices of bread; top with second bread slice.
2. Combine eggs, milk, sugar and salt in a shallow dish.
3. Melt butter in a skillet; dip both sides of sandwich in egg mixture and brown each side in skillet until golden.

FINGER FOOD

Crêpe Sandwich Torte with Sour Cream Mustard Sauce

Serves 4

8 (8-inch) crêpes
mayonnaise (optional)
prepared mustard (optional)
¼ pound thinly sliced ham
¼ pound thinly sliced Swiss cheese

1 package (10 ounces) frozen leaf spinach, cooked, drained and cooled
1 cup egg salad
Sour Cream-Mustard Sauce (optional)

1. To build an 8-tier sandwich, place 1 crêpe on a plate for the bottom layer. As you build the sandwich, spread each crêpe with mayonnaise or mustard according to your taste.
2. Top first crêpe with half the ham and another crêpe; add half the cheese and another crêpe.
3. Add half the spinach and another crêpe; add half the egg salad.
4. Repeat layers.
5. Refrigerate 30 minutes before serving.
6. To serve, cut sandwich into wedges and serve with warm Sour Cream-Mustard Sauce if desired.

Sour Cream-Mustard Sauce

½ cup white sauce
¼ cup dairy sour cream
½ teaspoon prepared mustard
salt to taste
pepper to taste

Mix all ingredients together; warm and serve over sandwich wedges.

Florentine Submarines

Serves 4 to 6

1 package (16 ounces) frozen Broccoli Florentine (contains broccoli, carrots and onions)
1 loaf French bread or 4 garlic bagels

garlic powder
grated mozzarella cheese
½ cup dairy sour cream
½ cup mayonnaise

1. Cook broccoli according to package directions; drain and blot with paper towels.
2. Split and quarter bread; sprinkle with garlic powder.
3. Divide cooked broccoli into 4 portions; place each portion on a bread quarter or split bagel.
4. Top with grated cheese.
5. Broil until cheese is slightly brown and bubbly.
6. Meanwhile, combine sour cream and mayonnaise; mix well.
7. Remove sandwiches from broiler; top each with a dollop of sour cream sauce.
8. Serve immediately.

Taco Crescents

Makes 16

- ¾ pound ground beef
- ½ cup minced onion
- 1 package (1¼ ounces) taco seasoning mix
- 1 can (2¼ ounces) minced ripe olives, drained
- 2 eggs, well beaten
- 2 packages (8 ounces each) refrigerated crescent dinner rolls
- 1 cup grated Cheddar cheese

1. Brown meat and onion; drain.
2. Add seasoning mix; mix thoroughly.
3. Add olives; set aside.
4. When cool, mix in eggs.
5. Remove rolls from package; separate into triangles.
6. Place some Cheddar cheese on each, then spread with about 1½ tablespoons of meat mixture; roll up and shape into crescents.
7. Place crescents on baking sheet; bake in preheated 375° F. oven 15 minutes, or until golden.

Ensaimada Rolls

Makes 1 dozen large rolls

- 1 package active dry yeast
- ¼ cup warm water
- 4 cups unsifted all-purpose flour
- 1 tablespoon baking powder
- ½ teaspoon salt
- ¾ cup sugar
- ¾ cup margarine
- 6 egg yolks
- ½ cup evaporated milk
- 2¼ grated sharp Cheddar cheese
- melted margarine
- additional sugar

1. Dissolve yeast in warm water.
2. Sift together flour, baking powder and salt twice.
3. Stir ¼ cup sugar and ½ cup flour mixture into dissolved yeast; cover and let rise in warm place, free from draft, until doubled in bulk, about 20 minutes.
4. Cream margarine; gradually add remaining sugar until well blended.
5. Add egg yolks, one at a time, beating well after each addition.
6. Beat in remaining flour mixture alternately with evaporated milk.
7. Stir in yeast mixture; beat until smooth.
8. Turn dough out onto a lightly floured board; divide into 12 equal pieces.
9. Roll each piece out to an 8-inch circle; sprinkle each circle with 2 tablespoons cheese.
10. Roll circles up like a jelly roll; coil into a snail shape.
11. Place on ungreased baking sheets; cover and let rise in a warm place, free from drafts, until doubled in bulk, about 1 hour.
12. Bake in preheated 400° F. oven 15 to 20 minutes, or until golden brown.
13. Remove from oven; brush with melted margarine and sprinkle with remaining cheese and additional sugar. Serve warm.

FINGER FOOD

Walnut Honey Buns

5¼ to 6¼ cups unsifted flour
⅓ cup sugar
1 teaspoon salt
½ teaspoon grated lemon peel
2 packages active dry yeast
1 cup (2 sticks) softened corn oil margarine
1⅓ cups very warm tap water (120° F. - 130° F.)
2 eggs (at room temperature)
Honey Walnut Filling
confectioner's sugar

1. Mix together 1½ cups flour, sugar, salt, lemon peel and undissolved yeast in a large bowl; add softened margarine.
2. Gradually add very warm tap water to dry ingredients; beat 2 minutes at medium speed of electric mixer, scraping bowl occasionally.
3. Add eggs and ½ cup flour; beat at high speed 2 minutes, scraping bowl occasionally.
4. Stir in enough additional flour to make a soft dough; cover and let dough rest 20 minutes.
5. Turn dough out onto well-floured board; divide into 3 equal pieces.
6. Roll each piece to an 8-inch square; cut each into eight 1-inch strips.
7. Twist each strip and coil into a circle, sealing ends underneath.
8. Place on greased baking sheets; make wide indentations in center of each coil, pressing to bottom.
9. Spoon prepared filling into indentations, using 1 teaspoon for each roll; cover loosely with plastic wrap and freeze until firm.
10. Transfer to plastic bags; freeze up to 4 weeks.
11. Remove from freezer; place on ungreased baking sheets.
12. Cover loosely with plastic wrap; let stand at room temperature until fully thawed, about 1 hour 45 minutes.
13. Let rise in warm place, free from draft, until more than doubled in bulk, about 45 minutes.
14. Bake in preheated 375° F. oven 15 to 20 minutes, or until done.
15. Remove from baking sheets; cool on wire racks.
16. Sprinkle with confectioner's sugar.

NOTE: After shaping, let rise in warm place, free from draft, until doubled in bulk. (Unfrozen dough will rise faster than frozen dough.) Bake as directed.

Honey Walnut Filling

⅓ cup honey
1 cup finely chopped English walnuts
¼ teaspoon salt
2 egg yolks, beaten
1 teaspoon grated lemon peel

1. Combine honey, nuts and salt in saucepan; bring to a boil.
2. Simmer over low heat 3 minutes.
3. Gradually stir in egg yolks; cook, stirring, until slightly thickened.
4. Stir in lemon peel; cool.

DESSERTS

Cheese Blintzes
Makes 16

2 eggs
1¼ teaspoons salt
1 teaspoon peanut oil
1¼ cups milk
1 cup unsifted all-purpose flour
1 container (8 ounces) pot cheese or dry cottage cheese
¼ cup sugar
¼ teaspoon ground cinnamon
additional peanut oil
dairy sour cream (optional)

1. Beat 1 egg lightly in a small bowl.
2. Add 1 teaspoon salt, peanut oil and milk; blend thoroughly.
3. Gradually add flour, beating until smooth.
4. Pour 2 tablespoons batter into a hot, lightly oiled 6-inch skillet, tilting pan to spread batter; cook over low heat until set.
5. Remove from pan.
6. Repeat with remaining batter.
7. Combine pot cheese or dry cottage cheese, remaining egg, sugar, remaining salt and cinnamon; blend thoroughly.
8. Place 2 tablespoons cheese filling in center of each blintz; fold sides over toward center and roll up, jelly-roll style.
9. Shallow-fry in hot 375° F. peanut oil until golden brown.
10. Serve with sour cream if desired.

Ambrosia Pizza
Serves 8 to 10

1 frozen 9-inch extra deep pie shell
1 package (8 ounces) cream cheese
1 tablespoon grated orange rind
½ cup light corn syrup
1 cup cold milk
1 package (3¾ ounces) instant vanilla pudding mix
1 cup toasted coconut
1 orange, peeled and sliced
¼ cup seedless green grapes, halved

1. Remove pastry shell from pie pan; place on cookie sheet to thaw.
2. With hands, flatten and shape into 12-inch circle; flute edge and pierce with a fork.
3. Bake in preheated 425° F. oven 10 to 12 minutes, or until lightly browned.
4. Beat cream cheese until smooth in a large bowl with mixer at high speed.
5. Add orange rind; beat until well mixed.
6. While beating, slowly pour in corn syrup; beat until light and fluffy.
7. Beat milk and pudding mix in a small bowl with mixer at low speed for 2 minutes; fold into cream cheese mixture.
8. Spoon onto prepared crust; sprinkle with coconut.
9. Arrange oranges and grapes on top; cover with plastic wrap and chill.

DESSERTS

Strawberry Crêpes

Makes about 20 crêpes

1 cup all-purpose flour
2 tablespoons sugar
¼ teaspoon salt
1¼ cups milk
4 eggs, lightly beaten
1 tablespoon pure vanilla extract or brandy
1 tablespoon butter, melted
Filling

1. Combine flour, sugar and salt; stir in milk, eggs and extract, beating until smooth.
2. Cover and let stand in refrigerator at least 1 hour.
3. Heat a small skillet or 6-inch crêpe pan until hot; brush pan quickly with butter to spread batter completely over bottom of pan.
4. Cook over medium heat until lightly browned on bottom, about 1 minute.
5. Turn and brown lightly on other side.
6. Remove to waxed paper to cool.

Filling

3 egg whites
1 cup confectioner's sugar
½ teaspoon grated orange peel
¼ teaspoon pure vanilla extract
⅛ teaspoon almond extract
1 package (16 ounces) frozen whole strawberries (without syrup)

1. Beat egg whites; gradually add sugar, beating until stiff peaks form.
2. Blend in orange peel and extracts; fold in strawberries.
3. Place about 1 tablespoon filling on each crêpe, slightly off center; roll filled crêpe.
4. Place crêpes in a shallow ovenproof dish, seam-side down; bake in preheated 450° F. oven 5 minutes.
5. Sprinkle each serving with additional confectioner's sugar.

NOTE: Batter can be made in blender or food processor and it will keep nicely in the refrigerator. If you are pressed for time, prepare batter one day and make crêpes the next day. Cooked crêpes can be stored in freezer. Place a piece of waxed paper between each crêpe and overwrap with plastic wrap. Defrost before filling.

Pineapple Cake Roll

Serves 8 to 10

2 cans (1 pound 4 ounces each) crushed pineapple
1 cup light brown sugar
⅓ cup shredded coconut
¼ cup minced nuts
1½ teaspoons pure vanilla extract
¾ teaspoon ground cinnamon
¼ teaspoon ground cloves
4 eggs, separated
⅔ cup sugar
¾ cup sifted all-purpose flour
1 teaspoon baking powder
½ teaspoon salt
confectioner's sugar
Pineapple Topping

DESSERTS

1. Drain pineapple; reserve ¾ cup juice and ½ cup crushed pineapple for topping.
2. Combine in a mixing bowl remaining pineapple, brown sugar, coconut, nuts, 1 teaspoon vanilla and spices; mix well and spread over bottom of an ungreased 15 × 10 × 1-inch jelly-roll pan. Set aside.
3. Beat egg whites in a mixing bowl until soft peaks form.
4. Gradually add ⅓ cup sugar; beat until stiff but not dry. Set aside.
5. Beat egg yolks in a separate bowl until thick and pale yellow; gradually beat in remaining sugar and vanilla.
6. Gently fold egg whites into egg yolk mixture.
7. Sift flour with baking powder and salt; gently fold flour mixture into egg mixture.
8. Spread cake batter evenly over pineapple mixture in pan.
9. Bake in preheated 375° F. oven 20 to 25 minutes.
10. Loosen cake around edge; invert on kitchen towel sprinkled with confectioner's sugar.
11. Let stand 3 to 4 minutes; Roll, jelly-roll fashion.
12. Cool; garnish with Pineapple Topping.

Pineapple Topping

¾ cup reserved pineapple juice
2 tablespoons sugar
1 tablespoon cornstarch
½ cup reserved crushed pineapple
1 tablespoon shredded coconut

1. Combine pineapple juice, sugar and cornstarch in a small saucepan; blend well.
2. Cook and stir until clear and thick; stir in pineapple.
3. Cool; use to garnish top of cake roll.
4. Sprinkle with coconut.

Blueberry Roll
Serves 6 to 8

1½ cups fresh blueberries
¼ cup plus 3 tablespoons sugar
1 egg
½ cup heavy cream (about)
2 cups packaged biscuit mix

1. Wash blueberries; drain well.
2. Sprinkle berries with ¼ cup sugar; set aside.
3. Beat egg; place in measuring cup and add enough cream to make ½ cup liquid. Stir.
4. Add egg mixture to biscuit mix in a bowl; add 3 tablespoons sugar, blending well. (This will make a very stiff dough.)
5. Roll out dough about ½-inch thick in rectangular shape, about 8 × 10 inches, on a well-floured board or waxed paper.
6. Sprinkle sweetened blueberries evenly over dough; carefully roll up lengthwise.
7. Bake on greased baking pan in preheated 400° F. oven 30 minutes.
8. Serve warm or cold.

DESSERTS

Mona's Walnut Florentines

Makes 2 dozen single Florentines

¼ cup butter or margarine
¼ cup half and half
⅓ cup brown sugar
¼ cup flour
dash of salt

¾ cup finely chopped walnuts
½ cup finely chopped candied orange peel
½ cup semi-sweet chocolate pieces

1. Combine butter, half and half and brown sugar in a saucepan; heat slowly until butter melts.
2. Remove from heat; stir in flour and salt, blending until smooth.
3. Stir in walnuts and orange peel.
4. Drop by rounded teaspoonfuls onto greased cookie sheet, allowing room for spreading; flatten slightly with back of spoon.
5. Bake in preheated 350° F. oven 10 to 12 minutes.
6. Let stand a minute or two on cookie sheet, then remove to wire racks to cool, using broad spatula.
7. When cold, melt chocolate over hot water; spread bottoms of cookies with a thin layer of chocolate.
8. Allow chocolate to set before storing cookies.
9. If desired, cookies can be put together in pairs with chocolate between.

Nut-Filled Pastries

Makes about 8 dozen

2½ cups unsifted flour
1 cup margarine
2 egg yolks, lightly beaten
½ cup dairy sour cream

2 cups ground pecans or walnuts
⅔ cup dark corn syrup
confectioner's sugar

1. Place flour in a large bowl; with pastry blender or two knives, cut in margarine until coarse crumbs form.
2. Stir in egg yolks and sour cream until well mixed.
3. Turn onto floured surface; knead until smooth; cover and chill 20 minutes.
4. Stir together nuts and corn syrup in a small bowl.
5. Roll out half the dough at a time to ⅛-inch thickness on lightly floured surface, keeping remaining dough refrigerated.
6. Cut dough into 2-inch squares; put ½ teaspoon nut filling diagonally across square.
7. Moisten 2 opposite corners slightly with water; fold over filling overlapping slightly.
8. Place on cookie sheet; bake in preheated 400° F. oven 12 minutes, or until edges are lightly browned.
9. Cool; sprinkle with confectioner's sugar.

DESSERTS

Dessert Fruit Tacos

Serves 10

- 2 cups melon balls or cubes (cantaloupe, watermelon, honeydew)
- 2 cups strawberries, washed, hulled and halved
- 2 cups pineapple chunks
- 1 cup seedless green grapes, halved
- 1 banana, peeled and sliced
- 1 orange, peeled, sectioned and sliced in ½-inch pieces
- 1 kiwi, peeled and sliced
- ¼ cup confectioner's sugar
- ¼ teaspoon cinnamon
- 1 box (10 shells) super-size taco shells
- shredded coconut (for garnish)

1. Combine all fruit in a large bowl; chill.
2. Sift together sugar and cinnamon.
3. Heat shells according to package directions; lightly sift sugar mixture over inside and outside of heated taco shells.
4. Fill each shell with 1 cup mixed fruit; garnish with coconut.

Spicy Applesauce Ice Cream Roll

Serves 8 to 10

- 3 eggs
- 1 cup sugar
- 1 can (16½ ounces) applesauce
- 1 cup all-purpose flour
- 1 teaspoon baking powder
- 1 teaspoon cinnamon
- ¼ teaspoon nutmeg
- ¼ teaspoon salt
- confectioner's sugar
- 1 quart vanilla ice cream, slightly softened

1. Line a greased 15 × 10 × 1-inch jelly-roll pan with waxed paper; grease paper.
2. In a small mixing bowl, beat eggs at high speed of electric mixer 5 minutes; gradually beat in sugar and ½ cup applesauce. (Reserve remaining applesauce for topping.)
3. Sift together flour, baking powder, ¾ teaspoon cinnamon, nutmeg and salt; blend into egg mixture, using low speed of mixer.
4. Spread batter in prepared pan; bake in preheated 375° F. oven 15 minutes, or until cake is lightly browned and springs back when pressed with finger.
5. Sprinkle clean dish towel with confectioner's sugar; immediately invert cake onto prepared towel.
6. Remove waxed paper; roll cake and towel from narrow end.
7. Cool completely.
8. Unroll cake, trimming edges if desired, remove from towel, spread with softened ice cream, and reroll.
9. Wrap tightly in foil or plastic film; freeze.
10. Blend reserved applesauce with remaining ¼ teaspoon cinnamon; chill.
11. When ready to serve, cut roll into 8 or 10 slices; top each slice with applesauce mixture.

DESSERTS

Dubonnet Golden Tart

Serves 8 to 10

Dubonnet Golden Filling
Quick Butter Pastry
unhulled ripe strawberries
confectioner's sugar

1. Spread filling evenly in pastry; let stand at room temperature 1 hour.
2. Just before serving, dust tart and strawberries with confectioner's sugar stirred through a strainer.
3. Cut tart into slender wedges; arrange a few berries beside each serving.

Dubonnet Golden Filling

6 egg yolks
6 tablespoons sugar
⅓ cup Dubonnet Blanc
¼ teaspoon pure vanilla extract

1. With a wire whisk, beat yolks, sugar, wine and vanilla together in the top of a double boiler; place over hot (not boiling) water.
2. Cook, whisking constantly, until thick, light, smooth and increased in volume, about 5 to 10 minutes.
3. Turn into a bowl and allow to cool, whisking occasionally.
4. Cover and chill through.

Quick Butter Pastry

1 cup sifted all-purpose flour
2 tablespoons sugar
⅛ teaspoon salt
6 tablespoons butter
1½ teaspoons finely grated fresh orange peel
1 egg yolk

1. Sift together flour, sugar and salt; cut in butter until particles are fine.
2. Stir in orange peel.
3. Beat egg yolk with a fork; add to mixture, tossing with a fork to moisten all parts.
4. Gather into a ball; roll out on a lightly floured pastry board on a pastry cloth to fit a fluted tart pan with removable bottom (9-inch diameter, 1-inch sides).
5. Fit into pan, pressing dough well into sides of pan (if pastry breaks, just press it back together).
6. Bake in preheated 375° F. oven until golden, about 20 minutes.
7. Cool on a rack; while slightly warm, gently loosen at edges.

Raisin Star Cookies

Makes 3½ dozen

½ cup butter or margarine
1 cup sugar
2 eggs
1 tablespoon fresh lemon juice
1 teaspoon grated lemon rind
2½ cups all-purpose flour
1 teaspoon salt
1 teaspoon baking powder
Filling

1. Cream butter in the large bowl of an electric mixer; gradually add sugar, creaming well.
2. Add eggs, 1 at a time, beating after each addition.
3. Blend in lemon juice and rind.
4. Mix in sifted dry ingredients; chill.
5. Roll dough ⅛-inch thick on lightly floured board; cut into 3-inch circles.
6. Place a small amount of filling on center of each circle; pinch edges in 5 places to make points; fold dough over filling between points.
7. Bake in preheated 375° F. oven 12 minutes.

Filling

1¾ cups raisins
¾ cup water
½ cup sugar
1 teaspoon cornstarch
dash of salt
1 tablespoon fresh lemon juice
1 teaspoon grated lemon rind

1. Rinse raisins.
2. Add water; simmer 5 minutes.
3. Combine remaining ingredients; add to raisins.
4. Cook, stirring, until clear and thickened; cool.

Cheese-Date Fold-Overs

Makes 2½ dozen

½ cup butter or margarine
1 cup grated sharp process American cheese
1⅓ cups sifted all-purpose flour
¼ teaspoon salt
2 tablespoons water
Date Filling

1. Cream butter and cheese until light.
2. Sift flour and salt together; blend into creamed mixture.
3. Add water; mix well.
4. Chill 4 to 5 hours.
5. Roll dough to ⅛ inch on well-floured surface; cut with a 2¾-inch biscuit cutter.
6. Place 1½ teaspoons filling on half of each circle; fold in half and seal edges with fork.
7. Bake on ungreased baking sheet in preheated 375° F. oven 8 to 10 minutes.
8. Cool slightly; remove from pan.

Date Filling

1 package (6¼ ounces) chopped pitted dates
½ cup brown sugar
¼ cup water

1. Combine dates, brown sugar and water; cook over medium heat, stirring occasionally, until the consistency of jam.
2. Cool.

DESSERTS

Angel Waldorf Delight
Serves 8 to 12

1 large angel food cake,
homemade or bought

Fruit Cream Filling

1. Slice entire top from cake about 1 inch down; lift off top and lay to one side.
2. Cut down into cake 1 inch from outer edge and 1 inch from middle hole, leaving a wall of cake at sides and bottom; remove center with curved knife or spoon, leaving cavity for filling.
3. Fill cake cavity with Fruit Cream Filling.
4. Replace top of cake; spread with remaining cream mixture on top and sides of cake.
5. Chill 4 to 8 hours before serving.

Fruit Cream Filling

3 cups heavy cream
⅓ cup confectioner's sugar
¾ cup crushed pineapple, well drained

1 cup fresh strawberries, cut in halves
6 marshmallows, cut in squares

1. Whip cream and confectioner's sugar together until stiff.
2. Fold rest of ingredients into a little less than half the cream; spread remaining cream on top and sides of cake.

Baked Alaska
Serves 6

1 quart ice cream
1 baked 9-inch cake layer, homemade or bought

6 egg whites
¾ cup sugar

1. Pack softened ice cream into a bowl not larger than 8 inches in diameter; freeze until very firm.
2. Cover a stiff cardboard circle, several inches larger than cake layer, with aluminum foil. (This is both baking utensil and server.)
3. Place cake on foil.
4. Beat egg whites until foamy; gradually add sugar, beating after each addition. Beat until sugar is dissolved and meringue stands in stiff, glossy peaks.
5. Unmold ice cream onto cake layer, centering it carefully; completely cover ice cream and cake with meringue.
6. Place in preheated 450° F. oven until delicately browned, about 5 minutes.
7. Serve immediately.

NOTE: *If prepared a day ahead, freeze. Brown just before serving.*